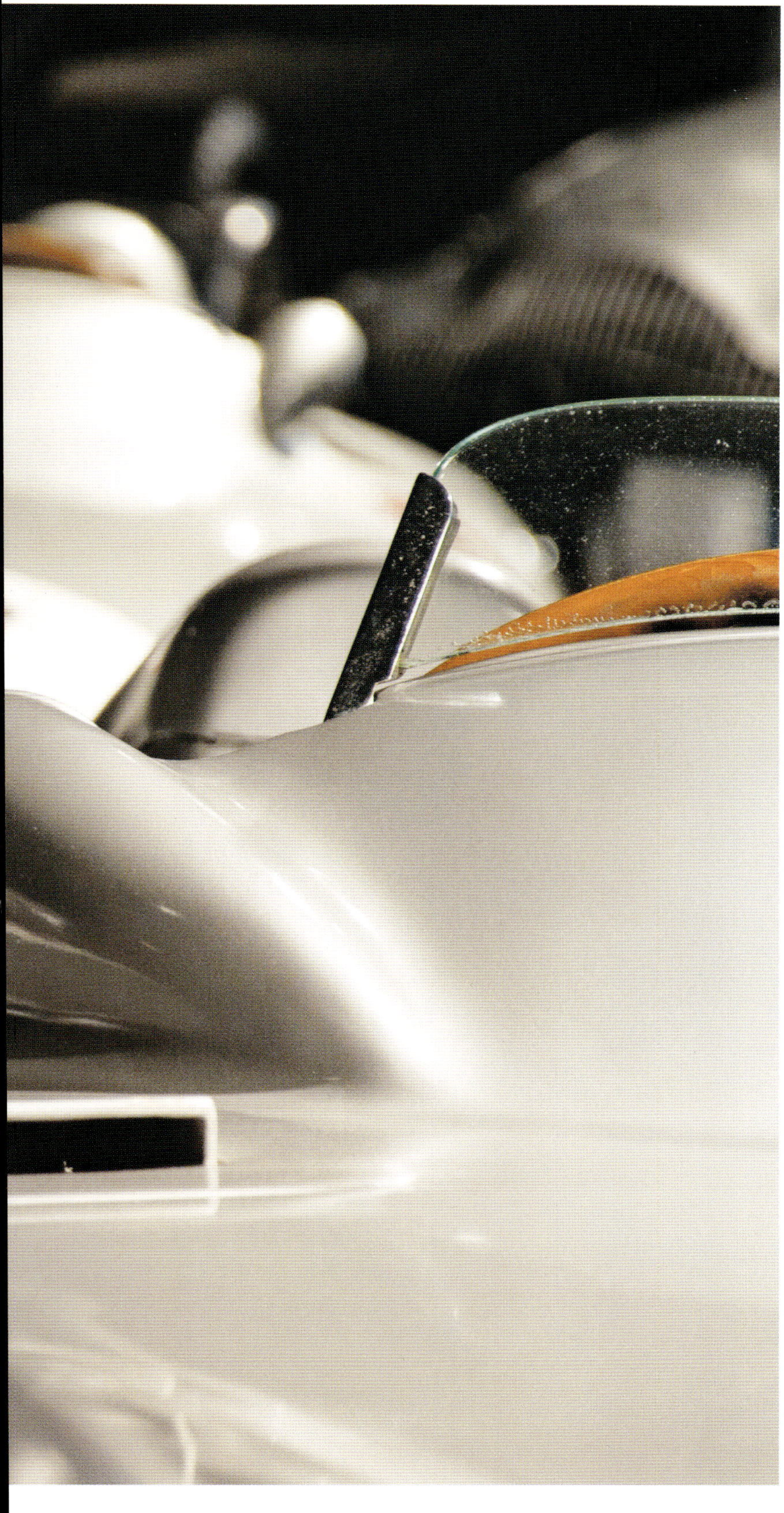

DREAM GARAGES
International

GREAT GARAGES AND COLLECTIONS
FROM AROUND THE WORLD

LEE KLANCHER

DEDICATION—To Steve Hendrickson

First published in 2011 by Motorbooks, an imprint of MBI Publishing Company, 400 First Avenue North, Suite 300, Minneapolis, MN 55401 USA

© 2011 Motorbooks
Text © 2011 Lee Klancher, unless noted otherwise.

All photographs are from the author's collection unless noted otherwise.

Front cover photo © Craig Lovell/Eagle Visions Photography/Alamy
Endpaper photo © Ingo Schulz/imagebroker/Alamy

All rights reserved. With the exception of quoting brief passages for the purposes of review, no part of this publication may be reproduced without prior written permission from the Publisher.

The information in this book is true and complete to the best of our knowledge. All recommendations are made without any guarantee on the part of the author or Publisher, who also disclaims any liability incurred in connection with the use of this data or specific details.

We recognize, further, that some words, model names, and designations mentioned herein are the property of the trademark holder. We use them for identification purposes only. This is not an official publication.

Motorbooks titles are also available at discounts in bulk quantity for industrial or sales-promotional use. For details write to Special Sales Manager at MBI Publishing Company, 400 First Avenue North, Suite 300, Minneapolis, MN 55401 USA.

To find out more about our books,
visit us online at www.motorbooks.com

Library of Congress Cataloging-in-Publication Data

Klancher, Lee, 1966-
 Dream garages international : great garages and collections from around the world / Lee Klancher.
       p. cm.
 Summary: "Some of the most amazing spaces in the world are profiled in this lavish, illustrated journey across the continents, fulfilling the automotive voyeur's dream of exploring private car sanctuaries from around the world. Incredible supercar collections, a museum packed with obscure makes and models, and quirky collector spaces from Europe, Japan, Australia, and North America combine to provide a fascinating portrait of how the gearhead phenomenon manifests itself in cultures across the globe"— Provided by publisher.
 ISBN 978-0-7603-4075-2 (hardback)
 1. Automobiles—Collectors and collecting. 2. Antique and classic cars—Pictorial works. 3. Garages. I. Title.
 TL7.A1.K58 2011
 629.222074—dc23
                                               2011031763

Editors: Steve Casper and Kris Palmer
Design Manager: Kou Lor
Designer: John Sticha
Cover designer: Rob Johnson, Toprotype, Inc.

Printed in China

10 9 8 7 6 5 4 3 2 1

CONTENTS

Introduction 7
Acknowledgments 175
Index 176

1 Exotic Collections 8
1 Mr. K's Lamborghini Dream 10
2 The Hungarian Hoarder 22
3 The Chicken Coop 32
4 The Mystery Man's Maserati Mahal 42

2 High-Test Nirvana 50
5 The Grand Prix Wizard's Private Portfolio 52
6 The Architect's Private Reserve 62
7 A Rock-Solid Kiwi Classic 70
8 The Hand-Built Honshu Hideout 76

3 Gearhead Geniuses 84
9 Pigsty Garage 86
10 The King of Kaponga 94
11 The Ferrari Fan 102
12 Barn Commandos 110

4 Sanctuaries 120
13 The Grand Prix Fan's High-Octane Den 122
14 Pilgrim's Playground 130
15 The Porsche Palace 138
16 Home of the Silver Arrow 146
17 Double Deco 156
18 The Beast of Budapest 166

INTRODUCTION

All garages house stories. The most common are beer-fueled bench racing spewed by the average garage-dweller—tales best enjoyed in person after the first 12-pack is dead and gone. Other garages house stories worth telling.

With this book, I and a crew of contributors found 18 unique and exceptional garages from around the world. Some of the stories come to life best through photography, and we let a few sing with minimal words and ample space dedicated to the visuals. Among these you will find elaborate palaces, visual tours de force that make your jaw drop and your head spin.

My favorites are those in which the owner has dedicated his or her life to hobbies housed within their hallowed palace. Such spaces are loaded with patina and those haphazardly beautiful creations of garage organization that spring to life after 20 years of living and working in a space.

Such places tend to accumulate cool things, ranging from spare SU carburetors to dusty magazine collections to oceans of stickers affixed to any flat metal surface in need of livelier décor.

I understand the allure of stickered tool boxes, spare parts useless to all but a handful of committed (committable?) enthusiasts, and pegboard lined with T-handles, torque wrenches, and new-old-stock brake pads. Many of my happiest hours have been spent in the garage, be it rebuilding the starter on my Husqvarna TE450 or throwing back beer and talking smart at garage-hosted Texas Hold'em and chili cook-off parties.

Well, now that I think about that, not all of my moments of gearhead nirvana occurred in the garage. I rebuilt a Chevrolet V-8 in my living room, and wrenched on my Honda CR250s in a chicken coop converted into a shop and, during the winter, in my basement. The point being that the mechanical joy that typically occurs in the garage can happen in any space where passion and wrenches intermingle.

The spaces in which new machines are created have a special vibe, an exciting air of gearhead innovation. The M55 garage in Budapest was such a place, a high-tech space that blended fastidiousness with stacks of hand-cast parts and cast-off test mules. Chris Cosentino's space in New Jersey (which is covered in *Motorcycle Dream Garages*) had a similar vibe, with parts, drawings, and engines scattered in intriguing corners.

I think to visit such spaces and people gets at the heart and soul of machine-oriented hobbies. Carefully engineered machines give off a tactile joy, from the wail of a perfectly tuned exhaust or the mechanical snick of a perfectly matched gearbox sliding into third. Walking into a space where rough-hewn test mules are sculpted into billet-slick finished vehicles is a trip into the forge, a look at how and why the cars and motorcycles we love to drive are created, cared for, and brought back to life.

—Lee Klancher, January 2011

part 1

EXOTIC COLLECTIONS

chapter 1

MR. K'S LAMBORGHINI DREAM

The Retractable World of a Japanese Enthusiast

FROM *GARAGE LIFE* MAGAZINE

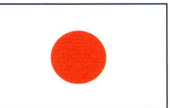

MR. K'S DREAM SOUNDED SIMPLE AT FIRST: to put his favorite Lamborghini Countach in the living room of his Japanese home. Such a dream makes perfect sense to those afflicted with cars; Mr. K just happened to have the wherewithal to actually make his dream happen.

While most car lovers are inclined to build a garage or basement *near* the living room to enjoy maintaining their cars and motorcycles, Mr. K went to the extreme. His plans were to build a system that would lift his favorite Countachs up to the living room on the second floor of his home. He wanted to literally surround his life with his cars. As one might assume, this was a costly project. The hardwood-topped lift alone cost $40,000, and the sliding floor cost another $60,000. The sliding floor completely covers the space for the lift and is also accommodated under the living room floor.

One of the first challenges to befall Mr. K (who wishes to remain anonymous) was that he wouldn't be able to use a normal maintenance lift, which would only have cost about $10,000 including installation fees. The maintenance lifts used in personal and commercial garages are not properly sealed and have entirely different construction components, so Mr. K needed a company capable of building a custom lift that would work properly inside a dwelling.

When he first started talking with construction companies about his architectural plans, he was declined again and again. But Mr. K. desperately wanted to appreciate his cars in this unique manner and persisted with his search. The plan was so magnificent and complicated that many companies were not at all up to the task. In the first place, nobody seemed to understand how this project would even be possible, and in the second, many wondered why he and his family would even want to be in a living room surrounded by Countachs.

Eventually Mr. K spoke with a Japanese manufacturing company. When he went to talk to them about his plans, he had no initial expectations, so he was shocked when they told him they could build what he needed. The company was capable of making custom lifts in any shape or size with no oil leaks, as well as lifts for commercial applications. According to Mr. K, the job of making a lift to carry up a Countach turned out to be a piece of cake for the company.

Years ago, when Mr. K was living in a condo, he had two cars parked at his building and two more parked in a lot nearby. At the time he had dreamed of building a house with a huge living room where he could admire his favorite Countachs.

Finally, in 2005 he had enough money and energy to make his dreams come true. After a lot of thought, time, money, and effort his dream castle was eventually completed. The entire place was custom designed by Takuya Tsuchida's No. 555 architectural design office. An alarm system called C-Bus2 handles security and also controls lighting.

Mr. K's Lamborghini dream currently resides in a nice quiet neighborhood in Japan. He says, "I am really happy and satisfied to be surrounded by my family and my Countachs. I couldn't be happier with the outcome!"

The floor of the living room slides back, revealing the Italian hardware in the garage.
Garage Life

The space is gorgeous—all you'd expect from an upscale urban home. The deep garage hints that wizardry awaits underneath the sleek exterior. *Garage Life*

Lovely machinery lurks under Mr. K's home, including this Ferrari 360 Spyder. *Garage Life*

Somewhere in Japan, a man—we'll call him Mr. K—his family, and his collection share a custom-designed space. *Garage Life*

> **I am really happy to be surrounded by my family and my Countachs.**

Above: Tools are stowed at hand in the garage. *Garage Life*

Top: Lamborghinis—particularly Countachs—are the favorites of our mysterious Japanese collector. This tidy system allows him to savor the exhaust note without poisoning his family with carbon monoxide fumes. *Garage Life*

Right: Windows downstairs offer a view of the cars. *Garage Life*

Facing page: Press a button . . .

Following spread: . . . and your favorite car can join you in the living room. *Garage Life*

A large living room and open ceilings offer spacious living by any standards. You may however, be forced to step around a Countach on the way to the kitchen table. *Garage Life*

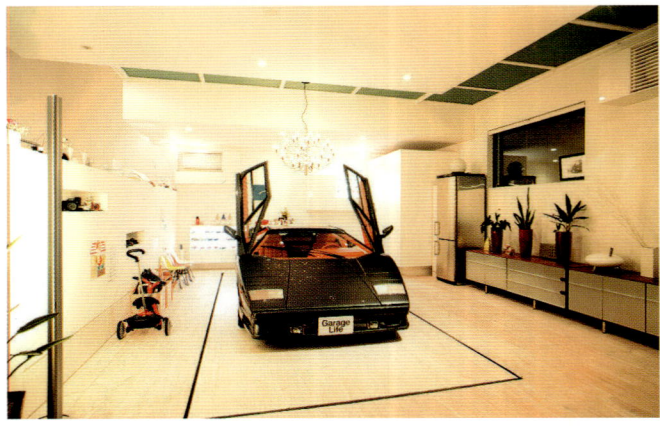

While most car lovers are inclined to build a garage *near* the living room to enjoy their cars, Mr. K went to the extreme.

The living space is open and beautifully designed. *Garage Life*

Shoes are left at the door, and slippers stand ready. *Garage Life*

Mr. K heads for the fridge. *Garage Life*

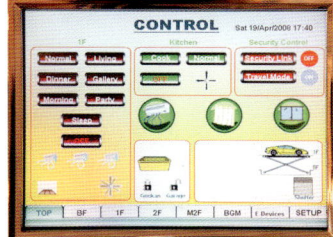

Computer controls handle the climate and the lift. *Garage Life*

A model collection is smartly displayed. *Garage Life*

chapter 2

THE HUNGARIAN HOARDER

22

The Movie Cars and War Relics of Oldtimer Park

SZILÁGYI MIHÁLY, WHO I CAME TO KNOW AS MISH, danced a Škoda Octavia through the narrow streets of central Budapest, juking and jiving traffic while firing off a nonstop monologue about the psychology of Budapest, his tenuous existence as a full-time blogger, and the complicated man and vast collection of cars we were about to visit.

"I'm sure he will let us see his collection," Mish said. "But don't prod. His past is . . . uncertain. So let me do the talking when we arrive."

I had met Mish in the modern way—via the Internet. While googling madly for Budapest garages, I found his website, Stipistop, a car-centric site named after a game Hungarian kids play, similar to Slug Bug but without the slugging. I found a few garage photos on Stipistop and sent Mish a note telling him I was in Budapest and looking for interesting garages to photograph. He responded, and less than 24 hours later we were careening across the city in a dual-fuel Škoda emblazoned with bright green lettering that read "30 PERCENT SAVINGS."

Mish promised to show me the most incredible collection of cars in Budapest. He sent me an aerial map of several city blocks covered with warehouses, makeshift tents, and row after row of cars, trucks, heavy equipment, and military vehicles.

A gregarious young entrepreneur, Mish built Stipistop into Hungary's largest auto-centric website. He is a natural salesman and innovator with a flair for the dramatic underpinned with the dark streak of self-criticism that reminded me, oddly, of people from my hometown of Rice Lake, Wisconsin. Whether the tendency is fostered by small places a bit off the mainstream or by landlocked regions of the world, residents of both tend to "throw themselves under the bus," as an old friend of mine likes to call my people's assumptions that they are at fault for most everything. I found this tendency prevalent in people from Budapest. I also had the good fortune of meeting some exceptionally talented, driven people from the region. Mish was one of those, and his mix of modesty and self-critical analysis were familiar and charming.

As Mish drove, he explained that the man we were visiting—Jankó István—had accumulated more than 170 cars and rented these cars out to film studios. The cars, he said, had appeared in many major motion pictures, including *Munich*, *Spy Game*, and others.

We drove into a gated yard that evoked a salvage yard or car repair shop. Cars were strewn amongst a battered collection of warehouses and sheds. Vehicles filled the interiors and lined the outsides of the sheds, grass growing up between wheels that hadn't turned in a half decade or more. The blustery gray November day accentuated the compound's industrial quality, and the air smelled of wet leaves, caked oil, and fermented gasoline.

We stepped inside the rusted trailer that served as company HQ, and Mish spoke with the woman at the front desk, an ill-tempered, Eastern European version of Edith Bunker. She told us István was busy and we would need to wait.

Mish and I went outside and wandered along row upon row of cars. In a series of temporary huts we found dozens of cars, most of them garden-variety Eastern bloc transport—Czech-built

A Russian-built 1962 Volga M21, a stylish little sedan that used a transmission based on a Ford three-speed. In 1956, a fleet of M21s were driven 29,000 kilometers across Russia in a highly-publicized effort to promote the cars.

Škodas, Russian GAZs, Volgas, and Ladas, and East German Trabants and Wartburgs. Among the unfamiliar makes lurked a large number of American and western European brands—everything from Volkswagen Beetles and Austin 1800s to GMC trucks and an AMC Gremlin. A smattering of ambulances built by Bedford, Citroën, and Nysa lay amid military vehicles from General Motors, DKW, and ZIL. István's tastes were nothing if not eclectic.

After about 40 minutes of wandering the property—and an education on Eastern European autos from Mish—we heard that István agreed to see us. A gray-bearded man of advanced middle age dressed in a brown oilskin jacket, striped brown tie, silver-horn-rimmed glasses, and a crisp white T-shirt, István gave off the air of a worn English professor who has spent a few too many long nights grading papers.

He invited us to join him in a tiny office jammed with the paraphernalia of the car addict—stacks of car magazines, literature, and documentation littered the space, along with a collection of gorgeous vintage radios. István offered coffee, served in a Styrofoam cup, and eyed me somewhat skeptically as I pulled out a notebook and, through Mish's interpretation, began to inquire what led him to this incredible collection of vehicles.

Before I could say a word, István had questions for me. Why did I want to see the cars? Where would I publish what I found? What kind of books did I write?

I explained that I profiled people who loved cars and motorcycles and that my books were for like-minded sorts. I said I preferred places that were built from passion rather than any kind of rationality. As Mish translated, István relaxed.

He told me that his collecting was something he couldn't explain or even quite control. "It's a sickness and a curse," he said, and I could sense that this teeming collection of cars was a burden for István. But the passion was as clear as the regret—his eyes lit up when he described acquiring one of his favorite cars.

István grew up in a small town north of Budapest, Hungary. Cars were not a regular part of life in his community. Under communist rule, owning things like cars and telephones was difficult. István recalled that only two people in town had cars. One was a doctor and the other one of the few individuals able to run a private enterprise in Hungary at that time. While communist rule forbade private enterprise, a few were able to get around this. István said that it was best not to ask about how those people were able to arrange for this.

István's father was an educated, well-read man who spoke seven languages. When Hungary unsuccessfully revolted against Russian communist rule in 1956, many prudent professionals left the country to avoid the strife. Not István's father. He had a giant collection of old books and couldn't bear to leave them behind. The family stayed on in Hungary and made it through the hard times of the revolution with the large library intact.

"In my family," István said, "collecting is a curse."

István didn't follow his father's path into book collecting. His obsession was cars. When he was four or five years old, his mother took him to the zoo. He had little or no interest in the animals. The cars in the parking lot, however, fascinated him.

His Austrian mother was able to acquire copies of the car magazine *Hobbi*. He pored over every copy and still has some of the magazines from 1958 and later in his collection.

He graduated from college with an engineering degree and took a job with Icarus, a growing Hungarian bus company. The company had just introduced a new series, the first of their buses to include an automatic transmission. The new models sold well, and István traveled around Europe, providing sales training for the new buses.

In 1972 he began to collect cars. His first was a Borgward P100. He bought more and more. While very few Hungarian people had cars at that time, money was even more scarce. The trick, according to István, was not buying the cars, but hiding them.

He stored his growing collection in gardens, tents, and sheds. People thought he was nuts. The genetic love of cars led István to continue to add more. And never sell any. He said that he had not sold a car in 25 years.

Jankó István's garage near central Budapest houses a collection of more than 170 cars distributed throughout a complex of warehouses, plus lines of cars in the open, sprawling over several acres. The 1957 Oldsmobile Golden Rocket 88 is the owner's favorite.

Facing page, top: Budapest is on the banks of the Danube River. The capital of Hungary was under communist rule until 1989. A few clever individuals managed to overcome the challenge of collecting cars at a time when private property was not quite illegal, but definitely not condoned.

Bottom: The Volkswagen Beetle with "Policia" on the roof (barely discernable) appeared in the movie *Munich*. The motorcycle is a sidecar-equipped BMW R12, and the Cadillac is a de Ville.

While he tended to purchase cars that evoked his childhood, he rarely met a car he didn't fall in love with. He particularly loved the big, finned cars of the 1950s, and he named an Oldsmobile Golden Rocket and Cadillac de Ville as two of his favorites.

When Hungary transitioned from communist to democratic government in 1989, István's hobby slowly became easier to manage. Owning property was no longer a dark secret, and he was able to pull his collection together.

Finding cars, however, became more difficult. István said that most cars had belonged to the government, and many of them were sold for scrap iron. As communist restrictions subsided, collecting cars for investment became more common. By the time I spoke with him in 2010, István said that most of the collectible cars in Hungary were in private hands and unavailable.

He began renting out his cars for use in motion pictures, photo shoots, and weddings. He claims to have supplied a blue Škoda 1100 for the movie *Spy Game*, several Volkswagen Beetles for *Munich*, and cars for several Hungarian films. He calls his business Oldtimer Park.

As István walked us through his collection, he told us how the cars tied to his childhood memories. When he was a kid, they were allowed to travel to a foreign country once every three years. The first time he went to Austria, his mother's family had a Borgward that captured his imagination.

He dearly hoped to purchase that exact car but was unable to acquire it. He did, however, buy another. He pointed to a line of buses in one of the warehouses and said that the buses reminded him of a childhood trip. An ambulance nearby reminded him of his father, who was taken to the hospital nearly every year.

"Through my cars," István said, "I am working my way through my memories."

István's eclectic mix derives more from what was available than any grand design. Cars from Eastern European bloc countries mix with brands from North America and Western Europe more freely than their owners did when the vehicles were built.

The orange and white 1956 Buick Special Riviera is flanked by a 1955 Škoda 440 Spartak. This room was filled with about 40 cars and stacks and stacks of parts.

The collection ranges from early touring cars to 1990s machines, with a heavy focus on cars from the 1950s. This room contains a 1978 Austin FX4 "London Taxi," 1937 Renault Celtaquatre, 1952 Mercedes-Benz 170V, 1952 Pobeda M20, 1955 Škoda, and 1968 Cadillac Coupe de Ville convertible.

Right: Parts are strewn all around the compound. For the knowledgeable, the place is a gold mine.

Below: This hulk of a VW Beetle carries the original plate under the remains of the hood.

Bottom: A 1939 Opel Blitz and a 1941 Dodge weapon carrier. The Blitz served the needs of the German military in World War II. Opel was owned by General Motors, and, in 1938, 29 percent of Opel's Blitz trucks were sold to the German military. The Dodge also served in World War II, although without the Blitz's political controversy as it was fighting for the Allies.

Borgward was a German auto manufacturer founded by Carl F. Borgward, whose first product was a two-horsepower three-wheeled car, the Blitzkarren, popular for postal delivery. The Hansa 1500 (right) was introduced after World War II. Borgward continued to produce cars, including a few sports racers, until the company went bankrupt and was sold in the early 1960s.

> Under communist rule, owning things like cars and telephones was difficult. István recalled that only two people in town had cars.

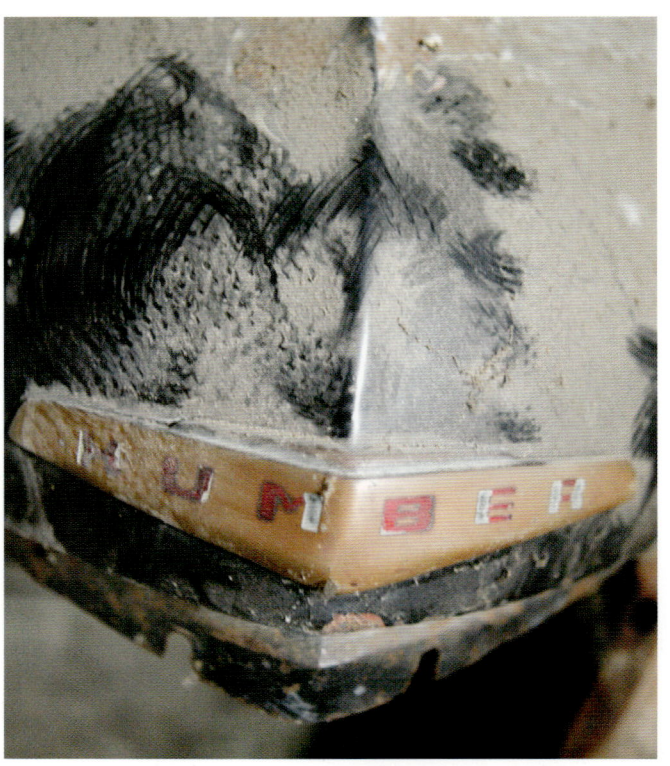

This room holds a bright blue 1975 Dacia 1300, which was built by a Romanian company that purchased the tooling for the Renault 12.

Left: István said this Chevrolet C60 was used on a movie set where it was shot full of .50-caliber holes.

Bottom: István (near driver's door) and his crew move one of the cars between warehouses.

Below: Narrow train tracks, now partly paved over, run right down the center of one of the warehouses, enhancing the sense of history, industry, and time's moldering hand.

chapter 3

THE CHICKEN COOP

32

Gordon Apker's Glorious Faux Farm

IN 1953, NINE-YEAR-OLD GORDON APKER spent most of his free time reading magazines and building models. The guidebooks to his obsession were *Rod and Custom*, *Popular Mechanics*, and any other car magazine he could lay hands on.

One of his favorite hangouts was Coy's Toys in Everett, Washington—a local model store where his mom would drop him off while she went shopping. A model builder rented the mezzanine above the store, and Apker would climb up the stairs to see what he was building.

"He just had a cornucopia of everything," Apker said, "and I was a model-building freak." His curiosity in seeking out and building miniature cars gave Apker a good foundation in the full-size machines emerging from Detroit, including special models created solely for shows and publicity.

Apker grew up at a time when American cars were the cutting edge of style. He was drawn to the sleek creations of the era, such as Harley Earl's luscious 1953 Cadillac Eldorado. Apker built every new car model available. When he periodically exhausted that supply, he filled in his time building battleships, aircraft, and anything else he could find. He would also, on occasion, ask the owner of Coy's Toys to look for his favorite new cars in kit form.

One design that especially captivated young Apker was an Oldsmobile concept car, the F-88. This roadster was one of the most popular and well-known concept cars of the day. Intended to compete with the Corvette, the high-performance Olds featured rocket-age styling and flashy, gold-flake metallic paint.

Gordon's fixation with cars stuck with him as he matured and entered the workforce, where his career followed an unexpected path. During college he took a job as a pizza cook at a Shakey's Pizza. His plan was to be a probation officer or to work for the FBI, but a chance arose to manage several new Shakey's stores, so he took it.

Shakey's restaurants were quite profitable in those days. By 1970 the group opened their fifth store, in Anchorage, Alaska. Apker was doing well enough that he drove a 1947 Oldsmobile (which he later restored) around to tour his little chain of parlors.

Also in 1970, Apker found an old farm for sale on the Puget Sound. The prime seven-acre piece was not cheap. He needed to come up with $40,000 for the down payment. He scrimped, begged, and borrowed less than that but enough to keep the bank happy. The place was his, complete with an old barn and falling-down chicken coop.

The owner offered to bulldoze the buildings, but Apker left them undisturbed. He had plans. "I wanted to build my garage," he said. "I knew someday I'd have cars."

By 1972 the barn was wired and plumbed. And filling up with cars. As Apker's situation improved, he added a few collectibles—first a 1933 Oldsmobile sedan, then a 1934 Ford flatbed and a 1936 Auburn.

"I wasn't buying them fast and furious then. In those days, you didn't buy a car for economic gain. We were just car guys. You bought what you liked. It was like owning a boat today," Apker said.

Gordon Apker made his way in the world as one of the key executives at Shakey's Pizza, but he made his name by selling a 1954 Olds F-88 concept car at the Barrett-Jackson Auction for $3.24 million in 2004.

Apker's 18,500-square-foot garage looks like an old barn when you drive up, but it has full-on dioramas and about 25 collectible cars inside. Apker calls it "The Chicken Coop."

Gordon Apker's seven-acre place on the water near downtown Seattle was once a farm, and Apker worked hard to retain its rustic appearance.

From 1974 to 1976, Apker and Claudia, his wife, began construction of a new home on the property. Apker hired one crew to work on both the garage and the home. He then put them to work building Shakey's Pizza restaurants, which they could nail together in 90 days, when they weren't working on his property.

The home omitted no luxury, yet retained the look and feel of an old farmhouse. Although not exactly demure, the walk-up does nothing to announce the nearly 8,000 square feet of living space inside.

Apker had the garage built in much the same way. His car collection was growing, and he intended to keep it at home among the tranquil old farm buildings. He used them, in fact, to hide the large structure housing his cars.

Along with the barn, the hobby farm had a small shed once used to house peacocks and other exotic birds. The only common thread between amassing feathered creatures and with collecting creations in alloy and steel are that they both like barns, though cars require a lot more space. Inspired by the similarity (or maybe the contrast), Apker and his wife, Claudia, dubbed Gordon's garage the Chicken Coop.

Assembling the collection to fill the coop took Apker on road trips to wherever nice automobiles could be found. Sometimes his journeys revealed rarer and more unique finds than

The waterfront property is tucked away a bit off the beaten path and has a distinctly rural feel.

> **Unless they are being restored, they are all in hop-in-and-drive condition. If I can't drive them, they are for sale.**

the ones that inspired the trip. Such was the case with a discovery he made in the early 1980s at a restoration shop called Sun Valley Classics in Tempe, Arizona. He had set off to view a 1933 Packard; once inside, a different car pulled him toward the back of the shop. It was just a shell, and yet its lines had etched themselves in his mind when he was still a boy. He could hardly believe it. This Arizona restorer had the body for the famous Olds F-88.

Apker called it out in delight but was surprised by the owner's reaction. "Who are you?" he demanded. "Who sent you here?"

When Apker explained his attachment to cars and his model-kit encounter with this very form as a child, the owner relaxed and opened up—a little. Getting a complete picture of all the shop owner had took a decade of Apker stopping by to visit and talk cars.

"At first, he said all he had was the body," Apker related. "But he had everything." The owner's reluctance to speak out was not centered on Apker. He was worried about General Motors, afraid they might try to confiscate the car if they knew it still existed. The rumor on the F-88 was that GM had destroyed it—they had destroyed the original chassis. What remained of the car was quietly crated and shipped to E. L. Cord, along with a stack of original blueprints and records and a partial parts list. Harley Earl procured a Corvette chassis for the car. According to Michael Lamm's detailed history, published in *Collectible Automobile*, the F-88 that Sun Valley acquired is most of the original car.

Sun Valley Classics had everything needed to reassemble the special one-off, and Apker wanted it, a desire he expressed on each visit to the shop's and car's owner. Meanwhile, the restorer was slowly putting the car back together. One day when Apker walked in he found the F-88 nearly complete. He asked the owner what was happening.

"Oh, I sold it," he replied. "Don Williams bought it. You wouldn't have paid me what Don Williams paid me."

Unfortunately for the proprietor and Apker, his assessment was likely wrong. Apker now owned 45 Shakey's stores and had resources to direct toward choice automobiles. The deal had been struck, though, and the Olds went to Williams. Apker tried to pry it free from the new owner to no avail. Incredibly, when Williams grew tired of it, he sold it to someone else.

"Gordie," he told Apker, "This guy paid me more than you would have paid me."

Luckily, Apker had something that Williams desired—and he wasn't parting with it unless Williams righted his earlier wrong. Apker would sell Williams the Bentley Speed Six he was after, if he could get Apker the F-88. This time, Williams came through, and Apker took possession of his elusive quarry in 1997.

Apker's collector companions thought he was nuts. One told him the F-88 wasn't worth more than $50,000. Their wisdom was wasted.

The F-88 was every bit as gorgeous as Apker had hoped—but it wasn't much pleasure on the road.

"As beautiful as that car is, it was that bad to drive," he explained. "I drove it, but it was one of those things that . . . it overheated quickly, steering wheel jammed right in your chest, the seat was super low with no padding . . . it was just not meant to go on the road."

In January 2005 Apker put the F-88 on the block at the Barrett-Jackson Auction, making a side wager with Craig Jackson. Apker bet the car would sell for less than a million dollars, while Craig took "over." Most of the car world knows that Craig won that bet by a wide margin. In a fierce bidding war that no doubt included men who'd built the same kit Apker had decades before, the uniquely styled F-88 netted $3.24 million—the highest price garnered for any car at the famous auction.

Moving the famous Olds brought in ample pocket change for additional cars. Apker maintains a rotating collection of about 25 vehicles, keeping another 15 or so in a 6,000-square-foot space in Arizona.

"Unless they are being restored, they are all in hop-in-and-drive condition," Apker said. "Man, if I can't drive them, they are for sale. That's what it's all about for me." The Chicken Coop is no roost for lame game.

This early 1950s Hudson Hornet is a beauty. The car's low center of gravity made it a popular choice for racing and sports enthusiasts of the time.

The door owner Gordon Apker is closing leads to about 40,000 square feet of garage space, all cleverly hidden behind an exterior carefully designed to look like an old farm.

Apker and one of his favorite cars, an early Packard, which was being prepared for a showing at the Pebble Beach Concours d'Elegance.

Right: The Kaiser-Frazer Corporation was a joint venture between Joseph W. Frazer and Henry J. Kaiser. The company built cars in the late 1940s until the 1970s, when AMC bought them. For a time, Kasier-Frazer built cars in the world's largest building, a structure in Michigan originally constructed by Ford to assemble B-24 Liberator bombers.

Far right: While Apker's collection has prewar as well as a few modern examples, the bulk of his machinery is from the 1940s and 1950s. The neon in the garage is as eye-catching as the cars. A Depression-era bumper car rests in the foreground.

The Kaiser Darrin sports car used a fiberglass body and was Packard's move to market and sell a successful sports car. Penned by

A Chrysler convertible sits across from a Rolls-Royce. The neon and wall mirrors give Apker's space the feel of a 1950s diner.

His curiosity in seeking out and building miniature cars gave Apker a good foundation in the full-size machines emerging from Detroit.

The front portion of the garage is the refinished interior of an old barn. The walls are paneled and floors carpeted, with a bathroom tucked in next to a few more cars.

Apker has an affinity for the Veltex brand, and his diorama contains what is most likely the world's most complete collection of Veltex-branded memorabilia.

40 Chapter 3

A 1938 Ford Deluxe woody station wagon. Very few of this model were built, and they are quite collectible today.

chapter 4

THE MYSTERY MAN'S MASERATI MAHAL

A High-Design Home for Exotic Speed Demons

BY CHARLES EVERITT

So, if you were a wealthy man of mystery, where would you house your Bugatti Veyron? I mean, you wouldn't park your 1,000-horsepower Molsheim monster, reputedly the fastest production car in the world, in some grotty little shed, would you? Nor your Maseratis (especially an MC12!), Maybach, Ferraris, or a Ford GT40. No, of course not. You'd want something fine and splendid, something designed by an award-winning architecture firm, the same that designed your home, right? And that's precisely what we have here, a magnificent car hole, if you will, created by DesRosiers Architects.

Man of mystery? Well, yes. Despite multiple impassioned entreaties, the owner simply refused to be interviewed. Something about a recent unpleasant experience with a magazine that left no doubt as to his identity put him off. Which left us with Louis DesRosiers, honcho of the eponymous DesRosiers Architects, as our sole line of communication. And, as you will see, this novel portal on our subject proved quite satisfactory.

To draft a soulful structure, an artistic eye and an inspired hand are not enough. You must understand what the building will house. DesRosiers certainly qualifies on both counts. A third-generation architect, DesRosiers and his firm have won 75 awards in the last five years from Detroit Home Awards; they also designed the first smart USA dealership in the country. Louis' first car was a '57 Chevy. He also had a 1959 Corvette, and he put a new engine into it himself. "I've had four Porsches for 12 years," he says. "We love those vehicles. I'm totally a car enthusiast. You can't be raised in the Detroit area without being a car buff. It's Motor City."

Our Mr. X selected DA in part because the firm had designed his original house and garage about 20 years previously. Continuity creates harmony. But the core reason DA got the job is a little more visceral—and says a lot about our unknown garage owner. "He interviewed three or four architectural firms," says DesRosiers, "and he said I was the only one who 'got it'—what his ultimate goals were. He liked our creativity and our passion for detail."

The client wanted another garage to accompany the existing one—and to match it, of course. He also wanted, well, a bit more. "He had 6 cars," DesRosiers says, "and wanted to house 14. The most important things were displaying the vehicles, plus a detail garage, designing the space for large parties, and having a penthouse [over the garage] for family and guests to use. The unique thing is it [the car court, or driveway to us plebes] used to be L-shaped; now it's U-shaped."

The completed space is just dandy for entertaining—let's say, more than 500 guests—and should they want to shake a leg, it will suit them dancing. It can be enclosed by a custom-designed tent. "We designed a tent, forty by forty," says DesRosiers, "and two stories tall. I had to design it so, if it rained, the water went into the garage drains. Plus it has air conditioning and heating. This is a very classy space for automobiles or ballroom dancing."

The garage itself is, as you can see, exquisite: clean, spare, and tasteful, and DA also renovated the existing garage across the breezeway to match, which, of course, it does

A man of mystery needs nice cars and a fine place to put them, don't you think? His Maserati MC12 keeps vigil outside, while two of its perhaps lesser kin stay snug and warm inside. *James Haefner*

Sumptuous materials—including a granite floor and a tricky mahogany wall system—characterize the interior, as does lighting that would do justice to an art gallery. Notice how neatly the garage doors are hidden when open. *James Haefner*

perfectly. There's an extensive mahogany wall system for storage, lighting that's perfect for displaying the owner's fine cars, and an elegant system for hiding the garage doors when they're open—one of DesRosiers' favorite details.

"I like the disappearing garage doors," he says, adding, "I would have put natural wood garage doors in instead of the stamped aluminum." Other favorites? "I love the floor textures," he says, "very classy, very clean. It's the overall quality of finishes in the space and the clean detailing. He wanted it to be as elegant as the automobiles."

Then there's the penthouse, a 1,500-square-foot space on the top floor of the garage where friends or family can stay. Expansive windows—including one 15-foot pane—offer magnificent views of the sprawling estate gardens and golf range. An elevator connects the main garage, detail garage on the lower level, and the penthouse, although there's also a soaring staircase from the garage to the penthouse, a signature feature of DesRosiers Architects.

So, that's what we know about this magnificent garage. What we know about the owner is, well, far less. He didn't even want to reveal how he got interested in cars. "He said, 'I don't want anybody to know that,'" says DesRosiers. Nor could we get a definitive list of his alleged 14 cars. We know from the pictures that there's a Veyron, various Maseratis (including a Gran Turismo and an MC12, of which only 50, supposedly, were built), a Ferrari or two, a Ford GT40 (the only American/Detroit-based car in the collection), and a Maybach, his daily driver—and little more.

"He likes fast, high-quality cars," DesRosiers says. "I'm sure his favorite car is the Veyron. He had an interesting phone call one day, 'Your right front tire is three pounds low.'" In the wireless age, a car of that caliber can speak for itself—helpful, especially with an owner who prefers not to.

Left: The garage is also home to the owner's daily driver, a Maybach, a true gentleman's express of luxury and swiftness.
George Dzahristos

Above: The owner plainly fancies Maseratis, as shown by this MC12 Supercar flanked by a brace of Gran Turismos. *James Haefner*

Following spread: The mystery-man owner clearly has eclectic tastes, ranging from the Ford GT40 (left) to the gem of the collection, a Bugatti Veyron, claimed to be the fastest road car on Earth. *George Dzahristos*

A breezeway connects the garage and upstairs penthouse with the existing garage at left, which was renovated to match the newer structure, also designed by DesRosiers Architects about 20 years ago. *George Dzahristos*

The back of the garage shows the copious windows, including the penthouse's 15-foot pane. The lowest level of the structure contains a vast detailing bay. *George Dzahristos*

Above: A penthouse above the garage features a 15-foot window offering expansive views of the gardens and golf range below. The 1,500-square-foot, two-bedroom penthouse provides a luxurious pied-á-terre for visiting guests. *George Dzahristos*

Top left: The men's room in the garage echoes the mahogany-paneled luxury of the garage itself. *George Dzahristos*

Top right: Dramatic, swooping staircases are a specialty of DesRosiers Architects, present and accounted for in the entry to the penthouse above the garage. *George Dzahristos*

part 2

HIGH-TEST NIRVANA

chapter 5

THE GRAND PRIX WIZARD'S PRIVATE PORTFOLIO

Giancarlo Morbidelli's World-Class Motorcycle Collection

BY PHIL AYNSLEY

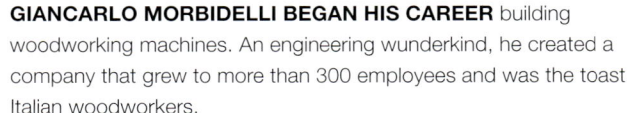

GIANCARLO MORBIDELLI BEGAN HIS CAREER building woodworking machines. An engineering wunderkind, he created a company that grew to more than 300 employees and was the toast of Italian woodworkers.

That business success gave Morbidelli the chance to pursue his real passion: building motorcycles. He started out in the late 1960s, crafting a series of innovative machines that won four Grand Prix championships in the 1970s.

When the Japanese invasion changed the face of motorcycling, the Morbidelli brand slowed a bit and nearly dropped from sight. To separate itself from the competition, the company designed a V-8 motorcycle with Pininfarina bodywork. The idea had more sex appeal than the finished product, however.

The 32-valve 850cc V-8 was a lovely jewel inspired by a Cosworth design. Output for the prototypes was an adequate but not overwhelming 120 horsepower at 11,000 rpm.

The engine's appeal was offset by the swoopy and futuristic 1980s styling, which failed to seduce writers and enthusiasts. Lacking sufficient beauty to derail buyers' sense of reason, the bike found no suitors at its $60,000 retail price. Only four prototypes were built before the project was abandoned.

Along with building bikes, Morbidelli began collecting them, assembling an enviable stable from his own and other factories across a broad swath of motorcycle history. In the 1990s he decided it was time to build a home for his collection. In typical visionary style, he created one of the world's most remarkable motorsports spaces, the Morbidelli Museum. The elegant space houses more than 250 bikes in Pesaro on Italy's Adriatic coast. Another 250 await restoration out back.

Beneath the soft lights stand row after row of historic machinery, including a line of Morbidelli's own creations. On the left is the first motorcycle Morbidelli built, a 125 two-stroke Grand Prix bike from 1967. At the other end is his company's last complete design, the 850 V-8 sports tourer from 1997. In the space of those 30 years he made his fortune in woodworking machinery, ran a Grand Prix team that won four World Championships using bikes of his own design, set up a factory (MBA) that produced competitive privateer GP bikes in quantity, and slowly continued to accumulate motorcycles.

Continue up the stairs at the Morbidelli Museum and the view is jaw-dropping. Four main halls house the bulk of the collection, which is laid out in chronological order—production bikes mixed with racing models in an ever-escalating ode to technological improvement. Each bike stands on its own mirrored plinth, so you can easily see parts normally hidden by fairings. Niches in the walls hold individual motors and other mechanical bits and pieces for further study. And most importantly, the bikes are generously spaced, so viewers can examine each one as closely as curiosity or obsession requires.

A view of the 1910s and 1920s hall. *Phil Aynsley*

Design evolution leaps out. The oldest bike on display is a 1906 Swiss Moto-Rêve with the night-vision technology of the time: a headlight shell with a candle in it. The most recent machine is a Ducati 851 superbike, with power, handling, aerodynamics, and brakes unthinkable in the Moto-Rêve's day. From the more than 80 years in between comes a smorgasbord of the everyday and the exotic. You don't see a 1942 vintage, supercharged 250/4 Benelli GP bike on every street corner. On the other hand, you used to see Honda 350 Fours there all the time. The museum has something for everyone—including a smaller room displaying all of the Morbidelli racing bikes.

Behind the main building is the busy workshop where both Morbidelli's own bikes, and those of like-minded collectors, are restored. A pair of 1950s vintage GP Mondials have pride of place at the moment.

Restoration is not the only work at hand. The master builder has a new creation underway—a mind-blowing 750cc V12! Designed to fit in a Honda CBR600 frame, this marvel of a motor is a side project sure to appeal to the high-tech collector. As Giancarlo says, on a subject he loves, "It is not the horsepower that is important. It is how it sings!"

The Morbidelli Museum is located in Pesaro, on the Adriatic coast. *Phil Aynsley*

Facing page: A view of one of the four halls that hold the majority of more than 250 bikes on display. This is truly one of the finest motorcycle museums in the world. *Phil Aynsley*

Left: Giancarlo still drafts the parts he requires to restore various old bikes in his collection. While there are more than 250 on display, there are a similar number awaiting restoration. *Phil Aynsley*

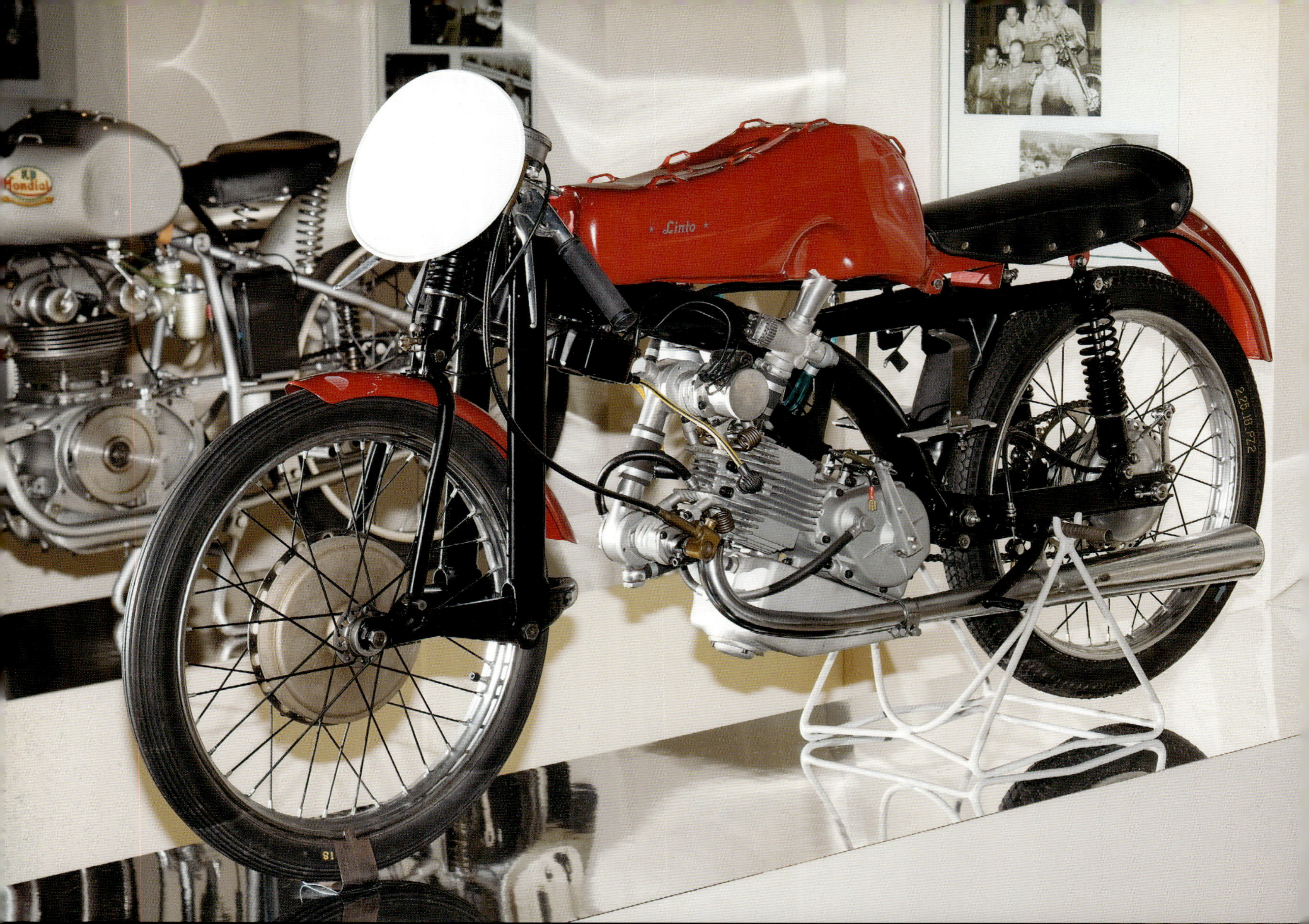

Linto 75 Bialbero (DOHC), 1956. 70cc 4-stroke single. 9 horsepower at 11,000 rpm. 95kg. 167 kilometers per hour top speed. *Phil Aynsley*

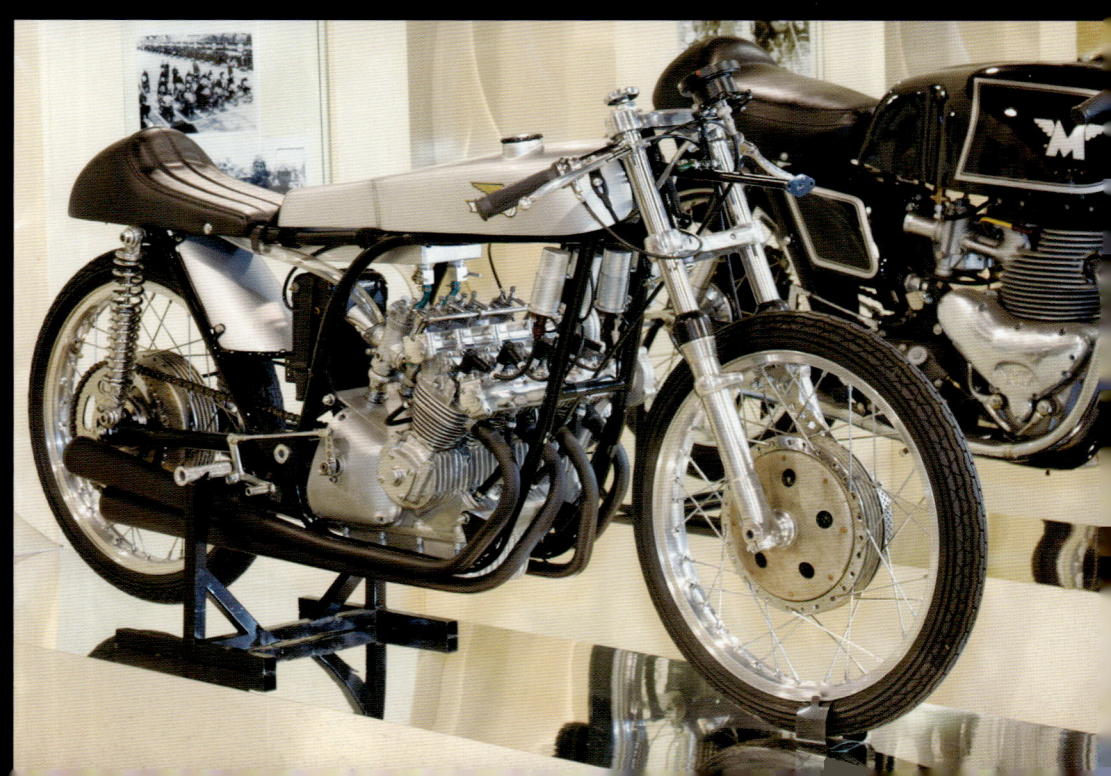

Ducati 125/4 GP. 1964. 23 horsepower at 14,000 rpm. DOHC, four valves per cylinder. Eight gears. 85kg. The motor of this one-off, Taglioni-designed Grand Prix bike (it never actually raced) resided in a Russian museum for many years before returning to Italy for a full restoration. *Phil Aynsley*

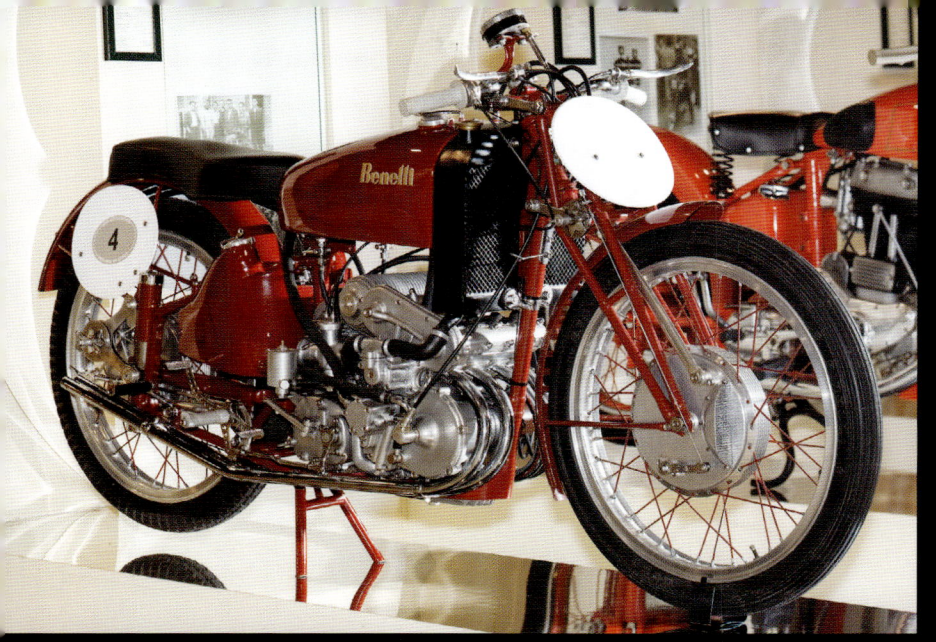

The museum has a large number of Benellis on display, Pesaro being their hometown. This 1942 Benelli 250/4 Supercharged GP produces 52.5 horsepower at 13,000 rpm, weighs 145kg, and has a top speed of 230 kilometers per hour. Developed during the war years, it never saw Grand Prix action as forced induction was banned when GP racing returned after the war.
Phil Aynsley

A 1969 Derbi 125/2 GP.
Phil Aynsley

Above: A Swiss-built 1906 Moto Reve 275, which produces 2 horsepower at 2,000 rpm and has a 50-kilometer-per-hour top speed. This elegant machine's lighting left a little to be desired. *Phil Aynsley*

Right: A 1919 ABC Skootamota 125. This English-built early scooter required manual pumping of the total-loss oil system. *Phil Aynsley*

Below: A smaller fifth hall holds most of Morbidelli's own machines. This group includes everything from 125 two-stroke single GP bikes to a 500 two-stroke square four. *Phil Aynsley*

A view of the 1940s and 1950s hall. *Phil Aynsley*

An impressive line up of Moto Guzzi singles, fronted by a 1926 500 two-valve Corsa. The engine makes 17 horsepower at 4,200 rpm. The bike weighs 130kg and has a top speed of 120 kilometers per hour. This model sold for a total price of 9,200 lire in Italy when released. *Phil Aynsley*

A pair of Mondial GP bikes undergoes painstaking restoration for their American owner. *Phil Aynsley*

Right: The wooden mock-up of the V12 750. *Phil Aynsley*

Below: Giancarlo Morbidelli's latest passion is a 750cc V12. The engine was designed to be fitted in a 600 CBR-R frame. *Phil Aynsley*

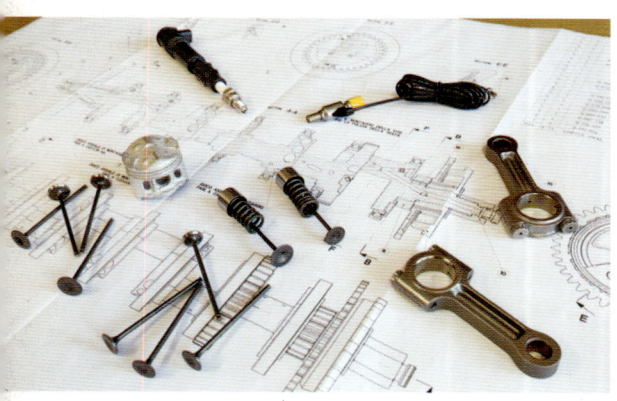

Flanking the entrance is one of the few production versions of the Morbidelli V8. *Phil Aynsley*

Also at the entrance is the very first machine Morbidelli produced: a 125 two-stroke GP bike. *Phil Aynsley*

chapter 6

THE ARCHITECT'S PRIVATE RESERVE

62

Bob Wirth's Hand-Built Garage and Collection

 **ON A SATURDAY NIGHT IN 1962,** Bob Wirth was standing at the bar during his 10th high school reunion with Jack, an old friend he hadn't seen since their student days. Jack mentioned he had a problem. He had recently purchased a Model A station wagon and also owned a Model T. Jack's home in Wawatosa, Wisconsin, had a one-car garage, so one of the cars had to go.

Wirth's father, who had passed away less than a year earlier, had always wanted to own a Model T but never found the time. Wirth was struck with the notion that perhaps he might fulfill his father's wish, by proxy.

"Jack," he said, "I'll buy that Model T."

He stopped by Jack's place the next day and spent a few hundred bucks on a pretty much original car in rough shape. Wirth was working at an architectural firm, putting in the long hours needed to get his license. He and his wife, Alice, were also in the process of building their first home.

The car was shuttled from neighbor to neighbor for a while, crammed into sheds and barns while Wirth built his house and career. The house was started in 1964, and Wirth and Alice moved in after the house was completed in 1965. In 1966 Wirth founded an architectural firm of his own and started building a permanent home for the Model T.

One of Wirth's goals with the design was to maximize energy efficiency. He understood such topics intimately and even taught a course in energy-conscious design at UW–Milwaukee in the early 1970s.

One of his ideas was to improve thermal efficiency by minimizing the surface area of the perimeter, minimizing wind exposure, and facing the door side into the sun. Wirth wanted his garage to be economical to heat during the long Wisconsin winters.

The solutions Wirth found were to make the garage door open to the south, so the sun could melt the snow on the drive and also warm the interior through the windows or when the door was open. He limited wind exposure by digging the rear of the garage a few feet into the hillside.

The most innovative concept in the garage was the shape. A typical rectangular garage—or a ranch home—is not very energy efficient. The shape that offers the best ratio of exterior perimeter to interior space is a circle, which minimizes the amount of perimeter and reduces heat loss. Building materials don't lend themselves to circles, however, so Wirth built his garage in a hexagon shape.

To do so he had to design the trusses and support system from scratch. The first garage used a center 4x4 post holding up a dead rafter that supported the roof.

The exterior was covered with redwood shingles, simply because Wirth loved the look. The vertical roughshod covering weathers beautifully and makes the building appear as part of the landscape on the heavily wooded lot.

Robert Wirth is an architect from southern Wisconsin with a penchant for MGs and early Fords. His garage is a cornucopia of nicely restored machines and endless shelves, drawers, and walls stocked with interesting parts and bits.

Wirth built three of these hexagonal garages. The shape minimizes heat loss, and the redwood shingles give the place an organic look that blends nicely into the wooded lot.

"It's not a particularly practical kind of roofing," Wirth said. "Drying and moisture shortens [the shingles'] life. They tend to stay damp and don't last as long as you like. I just happen to like them."

That first building gave Wirth a space to park his daily drivers, a spot for his Model T, and room for a workbench, which was entirely adequate for his initial plans. But by the time the garage was completed, Wirth had joined the Model T Ford Club and found that his passion for cars was blossoming.

He was attracted to the brass-era Model Ts, so he bought a 1914. He added an MGB. "I was also into sports cars and sports car clubs," Wirth said. "I was hooked on several ends of the hobby—Model Ts and sports cars."

The second garage was built to accommodate the growing collection, and Wirth added a refinement. He wanted to eliminate the center post, so he contacted a friend who was a structural engineer. That friend designed six-sided truss suspended from a center steel post. The men built a jig and assembled the truss with nails, wood glue, and plywood gusset plates.

The design was not only sturdy but also easy to assemble. The trusses are relatively short—especially when compared to 24-foot trusses commonly used to build a rectangular garage—and two people can easily put them in place during construction.

Wirth did much of the construction work on the second building himself. He hired a mason to lay the slab and a small contractor to put up the garage. The latter made slow progress right from the start. "He showed up less and less as the summer went on. I was working full-time and started working on the garage nights and weekends. I taught my two kids and wife how to put wood shakes on and did the roof on a very hot summer afternoon."

Wirth's firm was growing, as was his family. His son, Todd, had a natural ability for mechanics. When Todd was in high school, Wirth bought a Model A roadster. "The car was the wrong color—green—and it didn't run very well," Wirth said. He and Todd planned to fix the car up, starting with an engine rebuild, most likely followed up with some new paint. Todd suggested to Wirth that rather than just pull the engine, they do a frame-up restoration.

Wirth agreed and went off to work, not giving it a second thought. That night, when he came home, he was shocked to find the Model A scattered in pieces in the garage. Todd had torn the car down completely in a day, apparently without marking a single piece.

Wirth was shocked, but fortunately Ford had marked the key pieces, so Todd's speedy disassembly was not a major setback. In fact, father and son found they worked well together. When the Model T was finished, it won several car show awards.

The last of the three garages was built in the 1980s, by which time the redwood siding that had been economical and plentiful in the mid-1960s was neither.

"When we built the last one, that kind of redwood was unobtainable," Wirth said. "I found a guy who had redwood planks that were 16 feet long and two inches thick and eight inches wide. They had been used to wrap some kind of tank, like a cheese kettle." The planks were cut down into shingles that matched perfectly, and Wirth purchased them for less than the cost of pine.

"That was perfect," Wirth said. "Reclaiming something that would have been scrapped, and reclaiming perfectly clear redwood that now would be incredibly expensive."

In 1990, Wirth was working hard at his firm, as he had done for his entire career. The firm was founded with two partners, and the two architects and one structural engineer primarily designed commercial structures for well-established companies—banks and offices—but they also did private residences and developments. Keeping the business running required plenty of work during evenings and weekends.

Wirth's garage is a testament to 50 years of car collecting. An MG TF 1500 sits next to an MG TC.

Facing page: Vintage Ford parts fill this wall.

A miscellany of automobile memorabilia on the tool bench.

At a skating party, Wirth ran into a member of the Model T Club who said he had purchased a 1915 English Station Wagon Omnibus to assemble and had now decided against it. Wirth was interested and first saw the project as a pile of parts in his friend's basement. The project included plans from England, and he found reference to the kit in *Dyke's Automobile and Gas Engine Encyclopedia*. Wirth felt the kit was a rare piece and an interesting challenge to restore, so he bought it.

The kit languished until Christmas 1990. Todd's present to Wirth would be for them to finish the Omnibus. Todd said he would work with his father on the project every Monday night.

The pair took to the work, assembling the metal portion of the car and building the wooden bus carriage from scratch. They completed the car in June 1991. The end result was a gorgeous creation that is quite unique, and Wirth knows of only one other just like it, built by a man in Illinois.

The Omnibus gleams quietly in the third Wirth garage, one of the stars of the collection. Stored safely below the custom-designed trusses and warmed by the efficient, low-perimeter design, it is a hand-built testament in a hand-built garage.

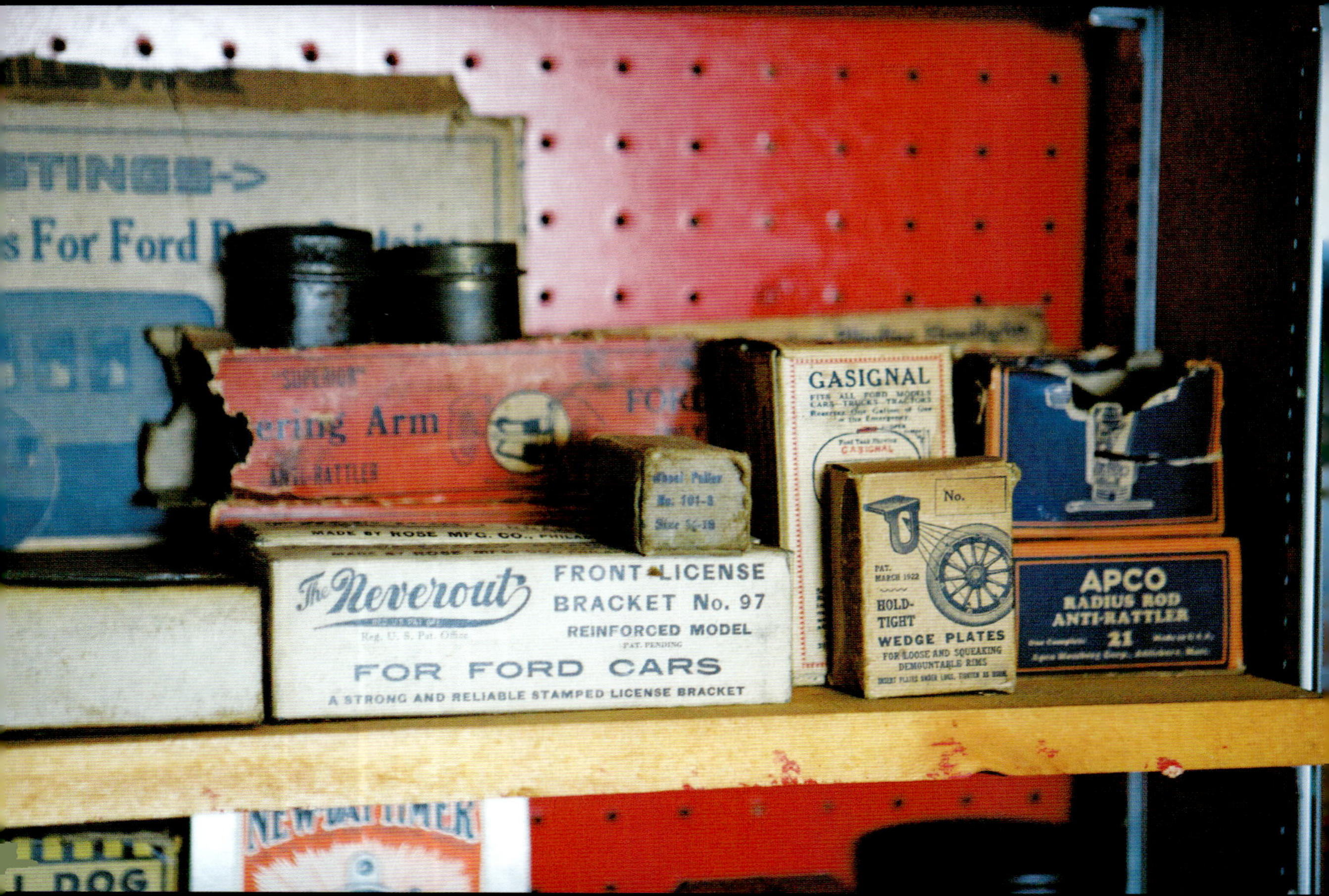

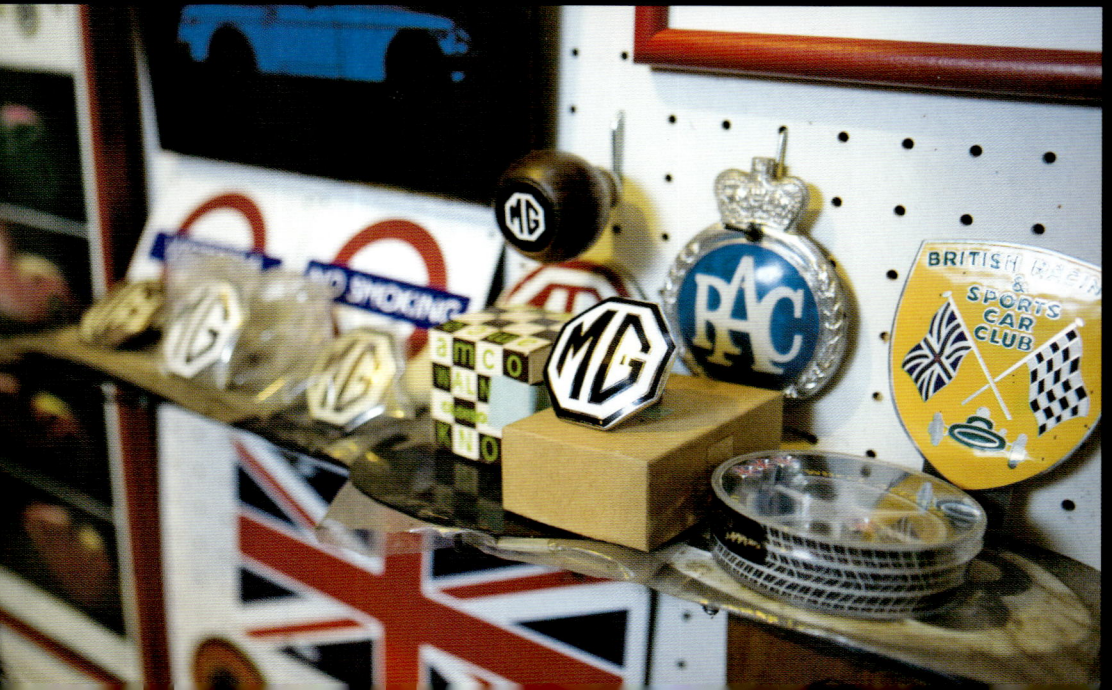

…The boxes for some of the parts take on a patina more interesting than the part itself.

While Wirth loves his early Fords, he also has a passion for British sports cars, particularly MGs

The upper garage was the second one built and the first of the three to feature a custom-designed roof truss that eliminated a center support post. Inside is a 1966 Corvair convertible, and a 1979 Porsche 924—both of these cars were purchased new by Wirth. Between them is a 1915 Model T English Station Wagon Omnibus restored by Wirth and his son.

A brass-era Ford, a 1909 Model T Touring.

The Architect's Private Reserve

chapter 7

A ROCK-SOLID KIWI CLASSIC

Roy Rook's Seven Decades of Repair and Restoration

BY GORDON CAMPBELL FROM *NEW ZEALAND CLASSIC CAR MAGAZINE*

NESTLED BETWEEN THE MOUNTAIN AND THE SEA, 20 minutes southwest of New Plymouth on New Zealand's Surf Highway, is the pleasant town of Okato. Once a thriving farm service center, the town has its own relaxed, slightly alternative character. A benign microclimate adds to its appeal as a delightful escape from the pace of the city.

For more than 80 years, Okato has been home to Ray Rook: garage owner, car enthusiast, and pillar of the community. Like many boys of the prewar years, Ray left school at 15 and took up a mechanic's apprenticeship at the local garage, Coastal Motors. There were 13 other mechanics, and they often worked double shifts. The owner was Charlie Maxwell, a gifted inventor and an almost impossibly hard boss. Ray bought the business in 1950, after he studied for a City & Guilds mechanical engineering degree and spent time in the New Zealand Air Force.

At the height of his success Ray had three busy workshops in Okato employing 22 people, as well as business interests in Auckland and Taupo. Coastal Motors grew from servicing and

Facing page: Rook's space is a simple and functional modified pole building with an office in the corner, recessed bays to work underneath the vehicles, and sides that open up to take advantage of the sea breezes. *Gordon Campbell*

While Rook ran three repair shops in Okato and the surrounding communities at the height of his business success, by 2009 he had closed all but the main shop and now only restores and repairs classic cars and trucks. *Gordon Campbell*

The town of Okato is just off the coast of New Zealand's north island. Ray Rook's one-stop repair shop, Coastal Motors, is an integral part of Okato. *Gordon Campbell*

Eighty-five-year-old Rook has lived his entire life in the town and has dedicated most of his years to servicing, repairing, and restoring cars. *Gordon Campbell*

repairs to engine reconditioning, interior re-trimming, panel-beating, and painting. Petrol and oil sales, breakdowns, and accident recovery were also part of the service and, as it was a country garage, any type of vehicle or machine was accepted.

Ray says he was strict with his painters—for good reason: he told his auto-body customers, "If you can see where we repaired your car, you don't pay." Ray is proud that his apprentices have all gone on to successful careers in the motor trade, many of them as business owners. Ray's one-stop restoration shop was years ahead of its time.

Lately, he has been winding down the business in response to changing times. He stopped doing panel repair when Japanese cars began to dominate and replacing the panel, or replacing the car, became the norm. He stopped painting about the same time as new technologies and regulations made it more costly. The abundance of Asian cars also killed the demand for engine reconditioning, so he sold his crankshaft grinding machine and other specialized equipment. Finally he gave up petrol sales and breakdown assistance, and downsized to one workshop.

At a young 87, Ray is semi-retired. He arrives late at the workshop and leaves early because he doesn't like to be late twice in one day. Tea breaks are longer than they used to be. He only works on classic cars and spends quite a bit of time resurrecting old ones that haven't run for 10 or 20 years. He says, "Every farmer on the coast has bought a classic car, mostly American," so there is no shortage of business.

There is plenty of variety too—for example, no sooner had he persuaded a Jaguar XJ-S convertible to run on all 12 cylinders than a local was dropping off a recently purchased 7.2-liter (440ci) Dodge pursuit car for Ray to get running. It wasn't a simple job because chunks had been cut from the wiring throughout the car, but it's all in a week's work. When I visited, he was gently bringing a Morris Eight Series E back to life.

One of Ray's specialties is building distributors for Model T Fords, a part that allows the cars to start more easily and run more smoothly. He retains the trembler coil for appearances and uses parts from Ford Tens and other models to make a distributor that is discreetly tucked away.

Two of Rook's favorite machines sit outside the shop in Okato: a 1967 Mustang and the 1948 Ford shop truck. The truck has been in service at Coastal Motors seemingly since time began.
Gordon Campbell

Ray says he is willing to depart from factory specifications on collector cars, but he does so for the best possible reasons.

Ray's personal fleet is an interesting mix. A 1948 Ford pickup has been his workshop truck for years and is well-known on the coast. His daily driver is an immaculate Ford Sierra Sapphire Ghia. There is the Subaru Leone 1800 coupe that his wife, Helen, bought new, and the rare fastback Hillman Imp GT that Ray purchased when it was just 650 kilometers old.

The pride of his fleet is a 1967 Ford Mustang he bought in 1969. Starting life with a polite 4.7-liter (289-ci) V-8, a Borg-Warner T4 automatic transmission and drum brakes, it was delivered to Ford's speed shop without turning a wheel on the road. Once there, it received an extreme makeover—with four-pot caliper disc front brakes, a Detroit Locker differential and heavy-duty axles, adjustable dampers, a T6 auto, and a 6.4-liter (390ci) V8 topped with a Paxton supercharger.

The original price tag of $2,400 increased to $4,700—a lot of money back then—but as Ray says, it was to Shelby specs, plus, and the supercharged engine flat-out rips.

The Mustang was brought to New Zealand by an American, ironically a "Mr. Holden," who came into the country regularly to work on the Glenbrook ironsand project. Ray bought the car and, as he had business interests in Auckland, he kept it there for the first year in case his farmer customers thought he had become too affluent at their expense.

He drove the Mustang daily for many years. It also saw quite a bit of competition in car club events—mostly hill climbs, time trials, and some circuit racing. In one flying quarter mile event Ray kept to a self-imposed limit of 5,000 rpm and recorded 239.3 kilometers per hour (148.7 mph) in one direction and 246.22 kilometers per hour (153 mph) on the return run. He knew the car was easily capable of running to 6,000 rpm, but the front end started to feel light at 190 kilometers per hour.

His most memorable race arose by chance when the family attended the Lady Wigram club car event during a South Island holiday. His club members pleaded that one of their cars was

The detritus of an automotive life.
Gordon Campbell

playing up and they needed another car and driver to compete in the teams event. It was a 50-lap all-comers race for sports saloons, and the last race of the day.

Ray protested that he didn't have race tires or a helmet, but that was quickly sorted out. In no time, the family luggage was sitting on the ground and Ray was lined up at the back of the grid. The other three team members started nearer the front with part fuel loads, intending to make one pit stop each. With a 22-liter auxiliary tank, Ray was sure he could do the 50 laps nonstop on a full load of fuel. The strategy worked, and he hit the front when the others pitted for fuel.

To his competitors' frustration, Ray slowed at each corner and used the Mustang's huge performance to blast down the following straight, keeping everyone behind him. This allowed his teammates to work their way through the field to catch him. The team finished one-two-three-four, and each received an engraved tray as a prize.

Ray completely rebuilt the Mustang with his son, Martin. After totally dismantling the car, they transported the body to Kiwi Metal Polishers in Rotorua to be chemically stripped. As each panel was finished, it was fully painted, so parts weren't left sitting around in primer. They ended up with seven shades of red and picked the one they liked best to repaint the whole car. Perfect panel joins and shut lines, difficult to achieve on an American car, are evidence of their care and attention to detail. Ray has refused invitations to enter the car in shows because he thinks it isn't good enough.

In a lifetime of cars, Ray still has fond memories of one of his first —a 1937 Austin 10 cabriolet, which may have been the only one in New Zealand. He drove it through the war years by modifying it to run on a mix of 18 liters of kerosene and nine of petrol. He would love to know whether the car still exists.

If you're passing through Okato on the Surf Highway, look for the blue-and-white Coastal Motors building on the main street. There is likely to be a classic car or two parked outside but, if not, it's still a great place to call in for a chat. It is one of those country-town businesses where the social aspect has always been, and still is, very important.

Ray Rook is one of those people who make mere mortals feel inadequate, and one wonders how he found time to fit everything in. Family, sport, community service—including 35 years as Okato's fire chief—business interests, deer stalking, overseas travel, motorsports . . . Ray's life has been a long and happy one, and he has packed a lot into it, although this list barely scratches the surface of his achievements. He is well-known and respected, and he makes time for everybody.

The bright sparkle in Ray's eyes and the hint of mischief in his ready smile are outward signs of time well lived. Ray Rook and Coastal Motors are true New Zealand classics.

Rook is a businessman and also an enthusiast. He has a long competition history that matches his shop history and has turned a wheel in rally, time trials, and roadracing events.
Gordon Campbell

Left: The Mustang carries a Paxton supercharger atop the 390-ci V-8 under the hood and enough other goodies to have recorded 153 miles per hour on a flying quarter-mile run. *Gordon Campbell*

Below: The 1967 Mustang has been his since 1969. The car served as Rook's daily driver for many years, and he also entered the car in car club events such as hill climbs, time trials, and roadracing. *Gordon Campbell*

chapter 8

THE HAND-BUILT HONSHU HIDEOUT

A Serious Enthusiast's Working Man's Paradise

FROM *GARAGE LIFE* MAGAZINE

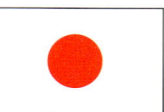

THE GARAGE IS A WONDERFUL PLACE TO ESCAPE, particularly for those whose finest hours are spent spinning wrenches. One man who has deep appreciation for the garage life is Kazuo Ueda.

He built his dream garage in the Mie Prefecture on Honshu Island, Japan in 1993. This is actually the third garage he has built. A popular saying in Japan is, "Do not get satisfied until you build three houses." For Ueda, that principle applied to his garages.

He built his first garage 30 years ago, sometime after he got his driver's license and his first car, a Mazda Rotary Presto. In 1977 he bought his second car, a '72 Rotary Cosmo. The inspiration behind the purchase of those first two cars came from his high school teacher, who was driving a Rotary Kapera Sabanna GT. Kazuo said, "That was the coolest car I had ever seen back then. I wanted to drive it so bad!"

As the years went by, the number of cars he owned continued to increase. He kept his Cosmo in his single-car garage, but he had no space for all the others and had to rent out monthly parking garages here and there. Of course his wish was to keep all of his cars in one location. At that point, he began contemplating building his own garage.

Today Kazuo is an architect. He is a representative for a company called Legendary House Nagoya, which is known for building old-style homes. When he started thinking about building the garage, Kazuo was just an employee. He had ideas but no money. One day a friend of his who owned a motorcycle shop was talking about opening a new place. The friend made an offer: if Kazuo designed a new shop for him, he would give him the old shop space for free. Kazuo quickly accepted the offer and acquired his first garage space. He used prefabrication methods to build his first garage castle and even built a pit to maintain his cars.

Ten years passed; he had hoped his first garage would last forever, but unfortunately the shop owner came back to reclaim his space. Kazuo knew there would never be a deal as perfect as his previous shop space. Reluctantly he rented out a warehouse space that cost him monthly rent and additional bills. At the time he could afford this, but he was sick of paying for something that he did not own. Kazuo then decided to buy some property and build his own garage.

He eventually found a space with about 10,000 square feet and started planning immediately. He planned to build the garage on the first floor and have a living space directly above it. Even though he was an architect, he was still on a limited budget. To keep the costs low, he decided to use inexpensive materials on the roof and walls and did much of the labor on his own. Trial and error ruled throughout the project.

To this day he jokes, "I never recommend to any customers to build a place the way I did. I did a lot of the basic construction by myself and was lucky to be an architect."

Do you remember the pit he had built in his first garage? Well, because it was underground there was a severe water leak. This time Kazuo decided to build a lift at his second shop to prevent the water problem. He found a lift at a shop that had gone out of business, removed it,

This compact space in the Mie Prefrecture on the island of Honshu was built by hand.
Garage Life

and installed it himself. Finally, his dream garage was built! These days Kazuo does not use the lift anymore; he eventually built a hair salon in the space.

One thing that complicated his search for the perfect location for his dream house and garage was the low ground clearance of his sports cars. He had to find a place where he did not have to drive over a sidewalk or curb to get into the garage. It was important to Kazuo to avoid scratching the underbellies of the cars.

Kazuo's favorite cars are old English cars, which are known for their propensity for oil leaks. With that in mind, a special anticorrosive epoxy paint was applied to the floor, and after 17 years the floor is still in great shape.

A section of his garage also serves as museum of antique collector's items. Zippos, watches, and all sorts of neat stuff cover the shelves and walls. Due to the fact that Kazuo has been gathering his favorite items for 40 years, there's plenty for visitors to look at. Although he has many valuables in his possession, Kazuo claims his hand-built garage is still the most important thing to him.

The cluttered space of a chronic collector, replete with the Van Jac brand and more. *Garage Life*

Mag wheels, tightly displayed and ready to roll. *Garage Life*

A Honda restoration project amidst barely streetable BMWs, Porsches, and a Miata. *Garage Life*

To this day he jokes, "I never recommend to any customers to build a place the way I did. I did a lot of the basic construction by myself and was lucky to be an architect."

Above: This Honda open-wheel race car is autographed and in perfect condition—and emblazoned with Ueda's favorite brand, Van Jac. *Garage Life*

Right: More Honda racing and street motorcycles, and another look at the Miata. *Garage Life*

Ueda is a hands-on collector, and his tool chest is well-stocked.
Garage Life

A collection of vintage Honda motorcycles and memorabilia fills one corner of the structure.
Garage Life

The garage was built by owner and architect Kazuo Ueda, an enthusiast with a passion for cars and motorcycles. *Garage Life*

The garage doors are adorned with murals, and the entry is designed to allow low-slung sports cars to enter without undue trauma to the undercarriage. *Garage Life*

> **A popular saying in Japan is, "Do not get satisfied until you build three houses."**

Above: Ueda and his family in his office. *Garage Life*

Left: The living quarters are what one might expect of an architect. This part of the house is now a hair salon. *Garage Life*

part 3

GEARHEAD GENIUSES

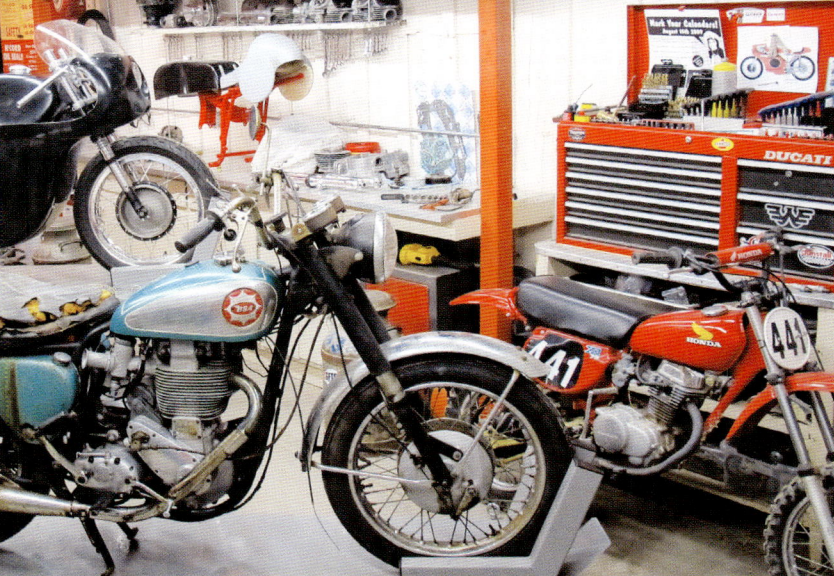

chapter 9

PIGSTY GARAGE

The Backyard Engineering Tale of Rob Collett and Fred White

BY MICK DUCKWORTH

FOR THE PAST 35 YEARS, Rob Collett and Fred White have been quietly working on an engine development program. Their production facility is an old pigsty at the bottom of Rob's garden, and their conference room is the pub across the road. One prototype "CW" bike, powered by several experimental single-cylinder engines built since the 1970s, is garaged in a lock-up round the corner.

"This is what old fogies do in their spare time," Rob laughs. "We've had some fun and games over the years. At our old place in Bedfordshire we were dyno testing on a Saturday and we got into trouble because the exhaust smoke was ruining someone's wedding photos. They said the noise had spoiled the service, too.

"Another time I made a big silencing chamber, but it filled with unburnt mixture and exploded. Fred was a ball of flame. His moustache and eyebrows were burnt off. It was quite a bang: all the neighbors came out."

Rob and Fred may be backyard engineers, but both have solid industry backgrounds. Before retiring in 1992, Rob worked for the Royal Aircraft Establishment and several big companies including de Havilland and Vauxhall Motors. It was at Vauxhall that he met Fred (real name Anthony), who is now a draughtsman with Cosworth Technology Ltd.

Rob is the ideas man, while Fred devises practical solutions. "You could call me the co-idiot," Fred says sheepishly. All the Collett-White engines built so far have a feature in common: a ported oscillating sleeve valve surrounding the piston. Sleeve valves on motorcycle engines date back to the Barr & Stroud four-stroke units fitted by several makers in the 1920s. In comparison with normal poppet valves, sleeves promised rapid port openings and unimpeded gas flow for long periods. In practice, they lacked the snappy response of normal OHV and OHC motors developed during the twenties, and there were snags with lubrication and gas-sealing. Still, colossal power outputs were achieved by supercharged sleeve-valve aero engines in the 1940s, and Rob believes the system still has potential.

"You can have huge port areas, and in a two-stroke the exhaust can be timed so that no incoming mixture is lost and wasted. You can experiment with lots of different configurations, and a big advantage is the ease of manufacturing on our limited equipment," Rob explains. "Also, we want to think laterally and do things that no one else has done."

His first sleeve valve engine was a two-stroke drawn up in 1973 and first run three years later. Originally envisaged as a 250cc twin with a six-speed gearbox in unit, it was built as a single-cylinder 125cc engine only. Induction was by a disc valve, while transfer and exhaust ports (12 of each) dispersed evenly around the bore were opened and closed by the sleeve. Like the Barr & Stroud, it used an eccentric and knuckle joint to operate the sleeve at engine speed, swiveling it in the bore as well as moving it up and down.

"We were concerned about adequate lubrication but found that with modern two-stroke oil we could forget the pump and run on 40:1 petroil mix [fuel and oil]." Road racer Steve Linsdell, who knew Rob through the UK vintage racing scene, took an interest. He encouraged the creation of

Fred White at the drawing board. He and friend Rob Collett run an engine development program in a tiny garage in Collett's backyard. *John Noble*

Rob Collett and Fred White built a unique sleeve-valve engine in a converted shed in Rob's backyard.
John Noble

The engine the two men have created is a sleeve-valve engine, a technology in which the air-fuel mixture and exhaust gas flows through movable ports in the cylinder sleeve.
John Noble

the next engine, an air-cooled 500cc four-stroke with a sleeve valve running at half engine speed, and provided a frame for road testing.

"It is much easier to make a cylinder head for a sleeve-valve engine than one with normal valves," Rob says. "But you are restricted in how far up the bore the piston can go without masking the ports, so you can't get very high compression."

The twin-plug four-stroke, tried with one, two, and three carburetors, was successful in that Rob covered nearly 10,000 road miles with it, but Linsdell did not see track potential in an output of 39 brake horsepower at the rear wheel.

"Four strokes are alright, but you can't beat the real thing," Rob grins. "We decided to go back to a two-stroke, which I always preferred. It offers much more scope for trying alternative port layouts."

Next up was a 500cc two-stroke with reed induction and sleeve-controlled transfer and exhaust ports, which covered a few thousand miles with occasional re-jigs in the 1990s. Ever eager to experiment, Rob and Fred added a mechanism to allow the valve timing to be altered by a cable control while on the road.

"That was a disaster," Rob says. "The epicyclical gear train broke up because small planetary gears had been accidentally overhardened."

Then came a two-stroke with traditional Schnürle loop gas flow instead of the uniflow pattern produced by radial ports. Also, the sleeve moved in the direction opposite that of the piston. That was followed by yet another design, reverting to all-round porting to give a mushroom-shaped gas flow.

"Neither of those two were very successful," Rob says.

The current MkV engine, begun in 2005, has the same built-up crankshaft supported on four ballraces with lip seals used since MkII. A casting specialist produces crankcases from patterns, all with a reed valve housing and uniform mounting points. A UK company supplies pistons, and the Weslake conrod runs on a 35mm needle-roller big-end. In the MkV, the EN9 carbon steel sleeve is moved up and down only by a small conrod on an eccentric running at engine speed. A Vernier permits changes to the sleeve timing in five-degree increments.

"Old sleeve valvers used the twisting motion to disperse lubricant, but we found we don't need that effect with modern oil," Rob explains.

The upper engine is a stack of aluminum sections machined in-house. A block resting on the crankcase incorporates the transfer ports, and the upper barrel bolts onto it, surrounded by a water jacket and the steel exhaust collector ring. The head, which protrudes down into the bore so that the sleeve surrounds it at the top of its stroke, bolts onto the barrel, and the top water jacket threads onto the head. The engine looks neat, but the hack bike as a whole is not so elegant. The frame was made for the four-stroke project by Steve Linsdell, influenced by the 1960s McIntyre Matchless Grand Prix design. An ultralow seat was envisaged, but for road use an MZ dual seat is plonked on at an unsightly angle.

A primary belt takes drive to a Norton four-speed gearbox via a Newby clutch. Linsdell planned to have the rear disc brake on a final drive countershaft at the swingarm pivot, so a short chain takes drive from the gearbox sprocket to the shaft, from which a second chain drives the rear wheel sprocket. The rear hub is a Royal Enfield cush-drive item.

A Norton front fork and brake are fitted, while various other cycle parts are MZ. The alloy fuel tank is from a Seeley racer and carries the creators' initials.

Another engine change is due in a few months when the MkVI two-stroke diesel engine is ready for test. There could also be further developments for earlier Collett-White engines, as they are being studied by a leading automotive company at a university laboratory. The four-stroke is of particular interest because of its possible low emissions potential.

"They have already paid for a new crankshaft," Rob says. "It would be great to see our ideas taken up and developed further."

> **Once we were dyno testing on a Saturday and we got into trouble because the exhaust smoke was ruining someone's wedding photos.**

Riding the Pigsty Garage Machine

I was curious to hear what such a strange engine would sound like. At tickover, it makes the *bung-bung-bung* sound you'd expect from a silenced two-stroke single, but intermittently, with regular pauses. Cruising along at 70 miles per hour in top, it sounds like a classic four-stroke single being hammered. There are no clanks or rattles, but it does vibrate moderately and would benefit from the rubber-bushed engine mounts usually found on two-strokes. The exhaust is remarkably smoke-free.

Throttle response is not fierce, but as the revs build up steadily, so does considerable torque. The soft character is not surprising in view of the small 30mm Amal MkII carburetor and a reed valve from one cylinder of a 250cc Yamaha twin, carried over from the original 125cc MkI. Present port timing is set for flexibility rather than sheer performance, and in deference to the low mileage I've been asked to be gentle.

A backward-facing indicator acts as a monitor light for the electric water pump, a Johnson marine type. I'm anxious when it goes out, but there's no sign of overheating and the switched pump still whirrs with the engine silent, so it's just the light. The battery, charged by an alternator chain-driven from the final drive jackshaft, also powers the coil-and points-ignition. The engine often kicks back when starting, but it's not as violent as a big four-stroke single can be.

Letting speed build through the gears rather than short-shifting, I find the CW an enjoyable bike with classic character. It is great for riding on rural lanes and roads, although the front brake could be better. I don't venture onto fast A roads or motorways, but I'd expect to cruise for mile after mile at 80 miles per hour, good going for an engine made in a pigsty.

A 40mm carburetor, bigger reed valve, digital ignition and tweaks to the sleeve timing and exhaust design would usefully boost performance. But Rob and Fred probably won't have time to develop the MkV: they'll be too busy getting their MkVI diesel up and running.

Reprinted from Classic Bike *magazine.*

The two men have built quite a number of engines during 35 years of development. Their running prototype is a bitsa assembled with a Norton four-speed gearbox, Newby clutch, Royal Enfield cush-drive hub, MZ seat, and other parts. *John Noble*

The Collett-White (CW) Mark V engine is a single-cylinder two-stroke.
John Noble

We want to think laterally and do things that no one else has done.

Collett is a former aircraft engineer for DeHavilland and Vauxhall Motors, while White was a draftsman for Cosworth Technology Ltd.
John Noble

> **Fred was a ball of flame. His moustache and eyebrows were burnt off. It wasn't half a bang: all the neighbors came out.**

Up Their Sleeves

American Charles Knight invented the sleeve-valve engine in 1903 to eliminate noisy and troublesome poppet valves with springs. His double-sleeve designs were used in several cars, including his own Silent Knight. A few years later single-sleeve designs were developed simultaneously by Scot Peter Burt and Canadian James McCollum; Burt's engines were built to power cars and aircraft. Glasgow optical-instrument company Barr & Stroud used the Burt-McCollum principle during its brief production of sleeve-valve motorcycle engines in the twenties. Their principle virtue was seen as mechanical silence.

English engineer Harry Ricardo studied sleeve-valve aero engines, focusing on problems around lubrication and differential expansion rates. His work led to the creation of the 3,500-brake horsepower, 24-cylinder Napier Sabre four-stroke and the Rolls-Royce Crecy V-12 fuel-injected two-stroke. Bristol made a series of radial engines with sleeve valves, culminating in the 3,000-horsepower, 18-cylinder Centaurus, which powered military and civil aircraft. All these designs used supercharging. The arrival of the jet engine halted development of high-powered piston engines for aircraft.

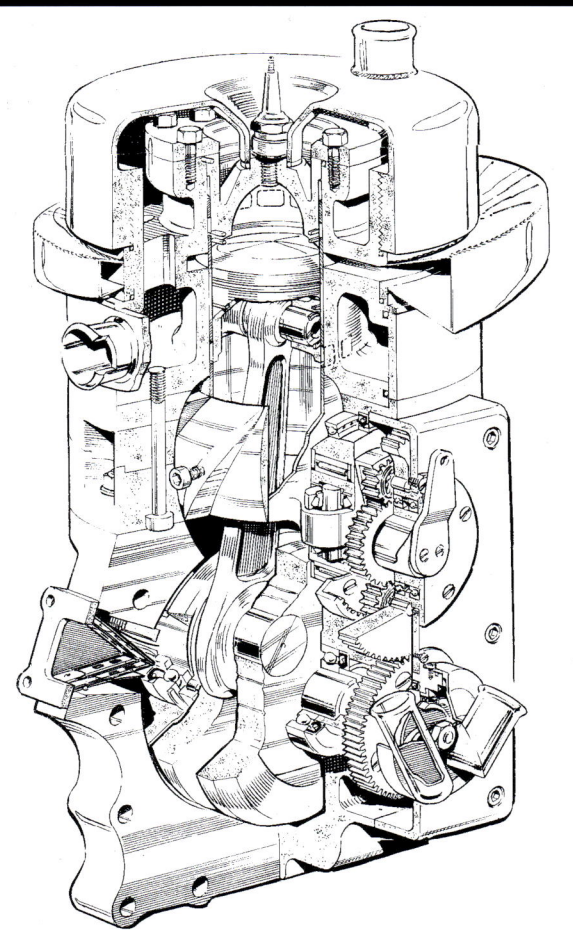

Above: The components of the CW engine are shown above. The CW engine uses modern technology to overcome some of the inefficiencies of early sleeve-valve engines. *John Noble*

Top: The supercharged 1,536-cubic-inch two-stroke V-12 Crecy sleeve-valve engine was developed by Rolls-Royce between 1941 and 1945. The engine returned more than 200 brake horsepower per liter but was never used in a production aircraft, as it was supplanted by jet propulsion.

Sleeve valve engines were used in early Daimler luxury cars as well as Bristol and other British aircraft. The early engines used excessive oil due to poor sealing, but modern designs are efficient with oil use and take advantage of the design's inherently high volumetric efficiency and high rev limits.
Rob Collett Collection

chapter 10

THE KING OF KAPONGA

Roy King's World-Class Restoration Shop

BY GORDON CAMPBELL

THE SLEEPY TOWN OF KAPONGA, NEW ZEALAND, on the slopes of Mount Taranaki, is a small place that houses a host of surprises. For years, the Kaponga Backgammon Club brought some of the world's top blues musicians to their clubrooms in a block of derelict shops. It wasn't uncommon for overseas artists to ask if they could play at the club.

Renowned restorer Roy King is even more of a Kaponga institution. Roy has been in the restoration business for many years and has never advertised. Work arrives by word of mouth and, like the musicians at the Backgammon Club, a lot of it comes from overseas. Kaponga may be an out of the way place to find world-class restoration skills, but it's Roy's home, and people who need his skills have no trouble finding him.

Roy almost never restores a complete car. His latest project is refurbishing a 1924 Fiat 519 chassis. When I first visited Roy, in late September 2008, his part in the restoration was nearing completion, and it was soon to be shipped to its Australian owner. The term "refurbish" hardly does justice to Roy's work over the last three or so years.

He received a very rough chassis and 54 boxes of scruffy parts. Roy cleaned and painted the chassis and fully overhauled the engine, gearbox, and differential before starting to make hundreds of irreplaceable items that were missing. The list of parts he manufactured is mind-boggling: fuel lines, wiring, wiring connectors, two splined rear hubs, four knock-off hubcaps, brackets, 40 grease nipples, and countless nuts and bolts, including 106 dome nuts.

Facing page: **King with his latest creation, a 1924 519 Fiat he has restored by hand-making parts.** *Gordon Campbell*

The motor engineering wizardry of Roy King takes place at this little shop in Kaponga, New Zealand. *Gordon Campbell*

A beautifully restored chassis in a tidy space. Gordon Campbell

The Fiat 519 chassis came to King in 54 boxes. The car is extremely rare. Produced between 1922 and 1927, about 25 are known to survive. Gordon Campbell

All six of the Fiat's unique spark plug caps were missing, so Roy had to make new ones, molding them from synthetic materials and casting FIAT into the top of each one. Making the mold, sourcing the right materials, and learning how to mix and mold them was an exacting process involving a lot of trial and error. He also machined the two-piece brass terminals that fit inside the caps.

At least he knew what the plug caps should look like. This project was his second Fiat 519 chassis restoration; the first was for a customer in Austria. Consequently, Roy is one of the few people who knows what the missing items should look like and where they should be fitted.

Roy couldn't buy the correct hose clips, so he made them – shaping the correct gauge wire, machining up the clamps and screws before having the parts nickel plated. He says there are nearly 1,600 nickel-plated parts on a Fiat 519 chassis, and yet it doesn't look overloaded with them. In its day, the 519 was a worthy competitor for Bentley, Rolls-Royce, Isotta-Fraschini, Hispano-Suiza, and others. Coincidentally, Roy has worked on an Isotta and a Hispano, as well as three other Fiat 519s, and he has a 1929 Rolls Twenty steering box, fuel pump, and gearbox in his workshop to be overhauled prior to assembling the chassis.

Roy's path to restoration renown came when he left school and signed on as a mechanic's apprentice at a garage at Auroa, South Taranaki. The rural garage serviced lots of vehicles, and working on cars was only a small part of the job. Roy found himself repairing trucks, tractors, and other farm machinery and doing general engineering. Whatever work came along, he did it. Cutting, bending, and welding pipes for new cowsheds in ankle-deep mud in the middle of winter was character building and valuable training.

At 18 years of age, Roy took up motor racing. Formula Vee founder Barry Munro sent him the rules, and Roy built a car, even though he hadn't actually seen one at the time. It was the fourth one built in New Zealand and the second to actually race—at the Paritutu circuit in New

Plymouth. That first race was in 1967, on the day Denny Hulme became world champion. From 36 starts, Roy won 18 races over three seasons before a desire to see the world took hold and he headed off on an extended overseas vacation.

From 1970 to 1972 he spent time in India and drove tour buses throughout Europe. He began the 1972 tourist season by flying to Istanbul, where the driver was ill in hospital and his bus had run its bearings. Roy paid to fly the driver back to England and set about fitting the new bearings he had brought with him. With the help of a local mechanic and three 10-to-12-year-old Pakistani boys who were living on the bus, Roy removed the huge AEC engine and gearbox from under the bus, working on the side of the road with "a hammer, screwdriver, and bottle jack." He took the crankshaft into Istanbul to be ground before reassembling the whole thing.

The arrangement with the tour company was that he kept the fares as wages, the company deriving its profits elsewhere. Roy filled the bus with paying passengers and arrived back in London with £300 in his pocket, more than half the price of a new Mini at the time.

Back in New Zealand, he bought Kaponga's run-down local garage and built up the business, expanding into tractor and machinery sales. In 1994 he sold all but the old garage and has been operating solo from there ever since, doing repairs and restoration work.

Later in his career, Roy restricted his paid working time to 40 hours a week, and a man must have a project in his leisure hours. Not surprisingly, it's a busman's holiday—he's building a replica of an early-1900s chain-driven racing car. This ambitious project is beyond the planning stage. The chassis is at the sandblaster, the engine sits in Roy's "showroom," and the Thorbensen rear axle/differential that will transfer the power from the gearbox to the chain sprockets is in his workshop.

The engine is a 7.4-liter unit from a Halley fire engine that served with the Onehunga Fire Brigade. He found the old fire engine in a hedge not far from his home and had to fell some trees to extract it. The Thorbensen rear axle/differential unit is from a Republic truck. A Greytown scrap dealer rescued it and passed it on to Ian Ridd of the Richardson Truck Museum in Invercargill. Roy had to negotiate with Ian, and it became his in exchange for a donation to the museum. The unit is a critical to the racer project because it has the 1.8:1 ratio he needs to get the correct gearing for the chain drive system, to give the car a top speed of about 160 kmh at 1,500 rpm. Another lucky find was a pair of hubs with large sprockets mounted on them.

Above: King's detailing is outstanding. Note the high-wheeler against the wall. *Gordon Campbell*

Top: A supercharger is tucked away on the side of the engine. *Gordon Campbell*

The lovely instrument panel on the 519. *Gordon Campbell*

The Marquette features a hand-built dash. *Gordon Campbell*

In earlier times, when his working week was more than 40 hours, Roy still found time for his own projects. In 1999 he built a pre-1920s racer-style car from a 1929 Marquette. Roy used a picture of a Mercer Raceabout to make scale drawings of his car, which he built during a year's part-time work.

The Marquette has been used frequently. Roy likes to get off the beaten track and drove the Molesworth Road and Danseys Pass among others during a 5,000-kilometer South Island tour in the company of two Bentleys. The car handles these roads with ease.

I had never been in (on?) a car as minimalist as the Marquette, so a short drive in the country was a unique experience. It was like riding a motorcycle, with the wind in my hair and no restricting bodywork. The 3.4-liter side valve six has locomotive torque and accelerates happily from 8 kilometers per hour in top (third) gear. Roy said it will travel easily at 120 kilometers per hour, but he kept the speed down to 70 to 80 kilometers per hour for our drive. Foot brakes and two handbrakes stop the car even better than it goes.

Roy offered me a turn behind the wheel but, having watched him deftly double-declutching his way up and down the gearbox, I made an excuse and stayed firmly in the passenger's seat. Travelling the country in such a car would be a lot of fun, but you wouldn't want to be the shy type.

After trying the Marquette, we went for a quick spin in Roy's Austin 7 Special. He surprised me by saying he didn't build the car. He bought it 30 years ago, just because he liked it. He has overhauled the mechanicals and added a few little extras (the huge radar detector wouldn't help the little car's power-to-weight ratio!), but otherwise the Austin is still as he bought it. The stubby

The Marquette Special is a 1929 Marquette converted to resemble a pre-1920s racer. The car is powered by a 3.4-liter side-valve six-cylinder and has both foot and hand brakes. *Gordon Campbell*

Speedometers, literature, tachometers, gauges, and superchargers decorate the walls of the King grotto. *Gordon Campbell*

little muffler on the left side makes plenty of noise, but Roy said the standard Austin engine produces very little power to match. He says it's the last vehicle he would sell.

Roy is still involved in motorsport. He's well-known on the North Island hill-climbing circuit, competing in the Chelsea, Ngawhini, Te Onepu, Pukeora, Kairangi, and other events, in the Austin and the Marquette. He takes pride in always recording the slowest time in the Austin.

Roy is a jack of all trades, capable of precision machining, mechanical repairs, electrical work, carpentry, painting, and many other tasks that are vital parts of the restoration business. He says the downside is that he can't become a true specialist in any one aspect and charge accordingly, yet he clearly isn't in this line of work for the money.

He is still relatively young, but the inevitable question arises of what will happen when Roy is no longer with us. There is no one to pass his skills on to, and it's difficult to imagine anyone else settling down to the difficult and time-consuming job of machining six rubber grips for Fiat 519 priming valves. Not many would want to machine 12 knock-off hub caps with the Fiat script on each one (he has another two sets to make for other cars).

Making hose clips or machining nuts and bolts would not appeal to many people, but Roy had no other option to ensure the car's details were correct. This attention to detail will greatly increase the value of the finished car, and its owner, Tony Ciccheillo of Brisbane, is lucky he found Roy. Tony had been over to visit several times, and he was back again at Easter for the first test drive with his friend and fellow 519 owner, Jeff Jones.

The car was finished, apart from the brass headlight shells, which are being repaired by Ivan Cranch in Auckland. Tony couldn't speak highly enough of Roy and his abilities. He is sure that no one else could have produced the same exceptional result.

After buying the Fiat seven years ago and putting it into a restoration of nearly four years, Tony was more than ready to get behind the wheel. The car drove very well, apart from a minor

King's work is mainly ground-up restorations of early cars, many of which come to him as boxes of parts shipped with partially assembled frames.
Gordon Campbell

fuel-starvation problem that wasn't evident during static tests. The original plan had been to fit a landaulet body, but Tony has decided to keep the car in its current state, exactly as it would have been delivered to the coach builder. Jeff noted that, for total authenticity, they would have to find a herring box for the driver to sit on.

Tony feels it would be a shame to cover up the beautiful workmanship and detailing in the chassis, and I agree. It's surprising that something so bare bones and functional can look so beautiful.

Roy is a collector who can't resist buying things that might come in handy one day. Some, like the Halley fire engine, are part of a plan, while others are stored or displayed in his showroom. His building is a treasure house. A BSA Winged Wheel, a Cyclemaster, and his daily Solex were among several motorized bicycles. A penny-farthing was leaning against a wall. A Royal Enfield 125 and Vespa and NZeta scooters will probably be sold soon. A Ford Model A awaits conversion to a "raceabout", while a Bradford just waits.

Roy is also a part-owner of a 1920s Benz (actually a Benz & Sohne), one of three left. He rebuilt the chassis and running gear from a heap of scrap, and it is now with the other owner to have a body built.

Roy has just completed his own Fiat 509 Roadster. Like the big Fiat, it started instantly and the engine ran like a clock. He intends to sell the car to finance the chain-drive racer.

Roy has a truly rare mix of skills and abilities, and he's thoroughly likeable in the bargain. Quietly spoken and unassuming, when he says, "I can build anything!" it's not a boast, just a simple statement of fact. If he doesn't know how to build it, he'll learn. As he says, "If it was made in 1924, it can be made today."

While Roy is happy to talk, he can also listen. He is very entertaining, and you dare not switch off in case you miss something. He's an interesting combination of the wisdom that comes with age and experience mixed with a boyish enthusiasm for life. His fund of knowledge and stories is vast. An afternoon with Roy passes very quickly indeed.

Having worked on some of the world's most revered makes, Roy says there is one gap in his CV—he has never worked on a Bugatti and would love to do so. If you have a Bugatti that needs anything from minor repairs to a total restoration, now might be a good time to contact Roy King.

—*Reprinted from* New Zealand Classic Car

The Austin 7 was one of the most popular prewar European cars ever built—a Euro contemporary of the Ford Model T. King's Austin 7 Special is one of many of the cars modified for sports use. *Gordon Campbell*

chapter 11

THE FERRARI FAN

John Pogson's Fantastically Red Refuge

BY NICK LAVIGUEUR

 **TRANSPORT YOURSELF BACK FOUR DECADES** to a little factory in northern Italy and you'll have some idea of what it's like walking in to John Pogson's garage. Time has stood still in this part of Yorkshire, England, and a scene not unlike Enzo Ferrari's original factory unfolds as you are overwhelmed by an array of classic Ferraris parked beside the shells of rare Italian supercars being lovingly assembled from the chassis up.

Three F40s line one side of the room while John's own immaculate 308 GT4 sits proudly gleaming amid a fantasy lineup few can match, on these shores or any other.

But this dream garage is no billionaire's vanity project; it is the realization of a childhood dream and the result of an epic journey from simple mechanic to one of the world's finest Ferrari minds. John's passion for and knowledge of the Prancing Horse marque is rivaled only by Maranello employees, making his Italia Autosport workshop the port of call for some of the country's most desirable vintage supercars.

The garage, launched more than 20 years ago, is famed for its attention to detail and restoration skills. The team's knowledge of Ferrari engineering has them doing anything from servicing old Testarossas to setting up F40s for some of the UK's most serious motorsport teams.

It's all a long cry from when the Huddersfield-born engineer trained as a mechanic in the early 1970s. In 1975 he got his first job at a Mercedes dealer in the town, yet within months he became fixated on the first Ferraris beginning to appear outside London.

"When a Ferrari came in to get its service, I made sure I was around," he recalls. "I then became the man for Ferraris. In the seventies Ferrari was young in this country, and I was young and I grew with it."

Millions of dollars of hot Italian metal call this place home today, including a 288 GTO, four 328s, a 1972 246 Dino GTS, a 1980 Boxer, a Testarossa, a 360 Modena Spider, a 456 GTM, a 355 GTB, a Mondial, and a 308 GTS quattro valve. And that's just the Ferraris. A 1964 Alfa Romeo Giulia Spider and a Lancia Fulvia sit on ramps awaiting their restorations, while a Jaguar XK120 flies the flag for Britain. Take a step across to John's storage garage and you'll find two more F40s and the last-ever Lamborghini Countach anniversary model in right-hand drive.

The appeal for petrolheads is easy to see. Where else would they Vaseline the roof and door seals on a 328 Targa, and where else has the boss raced to victory in a range of classic Ferraris that he set up himself? And indeed, where else could they tell stories of anonymous phone calls from Ferrari HQ and secret new parts being flown straight to their door? And what other garage across the breadth of Europe could tell you that the Formula 1 mechanic they hired didn't make the grade? The wall of trophies, plates, overalls, and jeroboams of long-since-sprayed champagne signify a racing ethic. These guys live and breathe nothing but Ferrari.

The old-fashioned ethos at work here draws in customers who know things aren't done by halves. The philosophy in this garage harks back to halcyon days when men made things with their hands; John draws his inspiration from his apprenticeship at the Ferrari headquarters in Maranello.

No that's not a reflection; that's three Ferrari F40s. *Andrew Catchpool*

"This garage is 40 years out of date," he boasts unapologetically. "We don't do things like the motor trade; everything we do here is old-school motor engineering, and we've carried that on through the decades. You repair a car as opposed to throwing parts away.

"In Northern Italy in the old days there was a factory where guys in baggy overalls and belts made something, and that is the way we have to work on these old cars. You are a craftsman working on an old car. Every one is different, because it was a different person who built it, and we have to dial in to that. We are an old-school garage, I'll stand on the roof and shout that."

It's wintertime, and John's team is working on what he calls a "last nut and bolt" restoration on a 200-miles-per-hour F40. The $700,000 car has been stripped down to its body panels, with even its washers being replated. Despite it being John's 31st year as a Ferrari mechanic, the work to reassemble the 470-brake horsepower racer has him buzzing like the very first time he cast his eyes on a glossy red 308.

"I get so excited," he says, "I've done it all this time, and I still get such an amazing buzz. It's like painting a picture. That's the canvas, and each component goes on and that's the painting.

"We're working with art, not cars. Quite often at a show you'll see someone staring at a particular area of a Ferrari. A 246 Dino is a beautiful car, but if you look at the roofline down to the rear buttresses that's a really nice angle. If you follow a Testarossa, the lines make it look like it's 16 feet wide and 2 feet high, and you can't believe it's going to fit on a road. Every model you can stand and you look at it and you see beauty in it."

Back in the 1970s and early 1980s John was the lucky youngster dispatched 200 miles south by his boss to pick up brand-new 308s and Boxers from the importer near London. He would then spend the day driving Maranello's latest masterpiece back to the Huddersfield showroom, giving him enviable time and experience behind the wheel of a host of what are now classic supercars.

"I was never short of girlfriends at that time!" he jokes. He describes driving a Ferrari as an "event" and still relishes test driving most of the cars that come through his doors.

"A modern car is designed to work easy, so it's not an event," he assures me. "But with a classic car, a 12-cylinder engine, you have to spend time with the machine.

"It's like starting an aircraft or a racing car. The ignition goes on and you hear the fuel pumps whirring away and they fill the carburetors, and then you hear the noise changes. Then it's time to pump the throttle; it's one pump for whatever number of cylinders you've got. That puts gas into the cylinders and it fires, but it doesn't start up smooth, it's all bang and crash. In some cases you just have 12 ram pipes, purple flames shooting out of the intake; it's like starting up an old Merlin Spitfire, and that is exciting.

"Eventually you get it on 12 cylinders and then you put the clutch down to take the drag off the thick gearbox oil, and you sit there on a high tickover and all the cylinders are clearing themselves and it settles down and a little bit of heat gets into it and then it's time to drive off.

"All Italian classics are the same whether it be a Maserati, Lancia, Lamborghini, or whatever; you never select second gear because it's tight because of the oil that's thick. So you miss second and you go from first to third and then eventually it warms up and everything's like butter.

"A modern person is going to say what a pain, but no it's not, because these are not cars, they're pieces of art—and that's an event." The sounds and smells also play a part in a package that has gripped John for more than three decades.

He adds, "This isn't a job; it's a way of life. We are so passionate about what we do. It's just a magical thing—the noise, what Ferrari stands for, it gets in your blood. In the seventies we believed that Ferrari employed a man just to get the noise of the engine right. Ferrari's V-6s are beautiful, but the F40 V-8 is the sweetest-sounding of all the V8s they produced.

Mr. Pininfarina at his best. This is a Ferrari 328 GTS, pre-ABS model. The wheels on a pre-ABS model have concave faces, and on an ABS model they have convex faces. "We think that Pininfarina-designed cars lost their way a bit after Enzo's days," says Pogson. *Andrew Catchpool*

Above: This is a $1.9M Ferrari 288 GTO. It was part of the prototype program for the F40, and you can see very crude prototype pipes, brackets, and other bits in this engine bay. *Andrew Catchpool*

Right: This 1978 308GTB race engine is fully overhauled and tested and will be shipped to serve as furnishing for someone's hallway in their home. *Andrew Catchpool*

Below: "It's not such a bad job. I have to come to work every day and see a line of F40s, engine covers up, looking like a series of reflections," Pogson said. *Andrew Catchpool*

"The V-8 goes back to the old 308s in 1975, and of course they're still using them in the 458, but the technologies romped on and different materials and rev ranges were used and now they scream.

"In the old days it was the carburetors, and you'd hear those more than the exhaust. I love to jump into a Magnum-type car and put the window down and listen to the intake, because I like to listen to the carburetors."

Pretty much every Ferrari has passed through John's garage, bar the £12m 250 GTO, but his staunch favorite is the 308, a car he still owns today.

"As opposed to the Magnum car, mine's a 308 GT4 2+2. I'm lucky enough to have found one that's been trapped in time for 31 years and looks like it's one year old.

"The reason I love it is because it brings back the memories of those days. When you drive it, it sounds, smells, and feels like no other car I've experienced.

"Inside you get real aluminum, real leather, and real stainless steel; there's hardly any plastic. I think it's an age thing. You do remember a period of your life; I remember that period of my life as being pretty special. I came into the Ferrari thing and I was in my early twenties and I was footloose and fancy free and that was a special time, and the noises and the smells of these old motorcars remind me of that."

John's passion for Ferrari goes beyond tinkering with the engine. He has also enjoyed a successful racing career both behind the scenes and behind the wheel.

As a driver he holds six championship wins, and he set up the same number for other drivers as a chief mechanic. He also holds 10 Concours d'Elegance wins on a host of Ferraris, including 308 GTBs and GT4s, F40s, and a 512 BB.

"It came about as a bit of a mistake," he says. "I'm an engineer, and I've had a racing license for many years because I build Ferrari racecars for clients. Rich people come along, and I build a really successful car, test it, set it up, and hand it over. . . . One chap said he was going away to America and suggested I race his car at the famous Spa circuit in Belgium. I went to Spa, and I actually won both races over the weekend. I do know how to set a motorcar up, and that gives me a great edge."

Having heard of his success, John's client let him continue racing, and he went on to win the championship in his debut season. The following year another client loaned him a 200-miles-per-hour Ferrari F40 supercar, and he won that championship too.

"People kept lending me their motorcars, and I kept winning championships, John recalls. "It was fantastic. The pinnacle was an F40 with massive horsepower, a proper racing thing, and I won a British championship against X220 Jaguars and big-horsepower Porsches."

Looking down on the workshop from his office, John reflects on his amazing life and says he is proud to have fostered what must be one of the greatest groups of car mechanics in the world.

"When I look down on the guys in the row of bays and there's a row of five F40s with their lids up, it's like a series of mirrors; that's how I like it. That's an amazing sight. When I look out there I see warmth. Every single one of those guys wants to come to work; that's the warmth and happiness of people, and I feel responsible for that, and that's a great feeling."

"GTO" stands for Grand Turismo Omologato. The 288 GTO was built initially for Group "B" racing, but they changed the rules, so it didn't race. *Andrew Catchpo*

Miniature exotica. Part of Pogson's vast collection of very expensive Ferraris. Shame they are only models! *Andrew Catchpool*

"The helmet in the background is my first helmet and I won two of my championships with it (1995 and 1997). The helmet in the foreground is my 2007 Alfa Championship–winning helmet. Sponsors have claimed my other championship helmets. You have no idea how many conversations I've had with myself wearing those hats whilst in battle." —John Pogson. *Andrew Catchpool*

The left racing suit was Pogson's first set and first championship in 1995. The black one was for the Ferrari F355 challenge. This was the suit he was wearing when he had the big shunt and fire at Donnington Park in 1998. The blue suit was year 2000, and the red and white ones won two championships in 1999 and 2001. Sponsors have claimed all Pogson's other race suits. "Some old race overalls of mine are hung up. Might I point out that there are no race boots hung up just yet?" Pogson said. *Andrew Catchpool*

Above: This is the bridge where the captain sits. The office chair is an old race seat from Pogson's F355 challenge car. *Andrew Catchpool*

Right: The captain in his chair. He said, "Thirty-six years fixing the damn things and I'm still smiling." *Andrew Catchpool*

An F40 engine bay. Note the catalytic converter model has silver airboxes, not black, and has a hump on the crossmember, shown in the photograph. This is where the "CATS" live. The car in the background is a 328 GTS. *Andrew Catchpool*

A Ferrari F40 that has been totally restored. The engine and gearbox have just been fitted back. "To me it looks just like a Group 'C' Le Mans racer from the eighties. I don't know about you, but I think unlike the German so-called equivalents, that this is automotive art," Pogson said. *Andrew Catchpool*

chapter 12

BARN COMMANDOS

The Super Friends of Classic Motorcycles

BY CHARLES EVERITT

IT ALL STARTED WITH MATTEL RRRUMBLERS MOTORCYCLE STUNT TOYS and a Lego Norton Commando model when Mike Watanabe was six years old. Those playthings sparked his interest in motorcycles, especially the ungainly looking Lego model. That's when he said, "I'm going to get a Norton Commando." It took almost 15 years, but he finally got that Norton—a 1973 Roadster. Since then, it has become a gleaming British endorsement for Watanabe's restoration and customizing business, Union Motorcycle Classics of Nampa, Idaho.

The original Roadster was a handsome enough beast, to be sure. Watanabe has transformed it, though, to more of a café racer style, largely through use of bodywork from UMC's longtime collaborators and allies, Glass from the Past, in Oregon. Now, it resembles some of the Dunstall Norton Commandos of the 1960s, albeit with a more modern and rounded seat unit. "I've always kept that one bike," Watanabe says. "I'll probably never sell that bike." It's easy to see why. His daily ride, though, is a 1993 Ducati 900SS, a custom somewhat similar to his Norton, but with a harder, racier edge. Yet the two share a certain café racer style that's more polished than usual.

A 1974 Montesa Cota 25, a 50cc trials bike for youngsters, illustrates another facet of UMC's capabilities: restoration and renovation. The Montesa is a tiny gem, restored lovingly—although perhaps *renovated* is a better word. Oh, it's complete, down to the Montesa logos on the fork and shocks, the badges on the nicely painted fiberglass, and even the footpeg rubbers. But it's not the clutch-one's-pearls perfection of a better-than-new, concours, 100-point full resto. Rather, the footpeg rubbers and period-correct Doherty-style grips are worn, the hubs (though clean) haven't been polished to a preternatural sheen, and there are dings in the fork sliders. In short, it's slightly funky. Not that UMC can't do a 100-point restoration. They just have a fondness for a certain patina of age.

That fondness is best represented by UMC's 1961 Triumph Tiger Cub, a fine, 200cc example of perfidious Albion underachievement, and the third facet of UMC's talents: leaving well enough alone. Where the Montesa is slightly funky, the Tiger Cub is decidedly so: the paint faded and flaking; the aluminum oxidized; the kickstart rubber shredded. The bike has a down-at-the-heels look and feel—but it's a runner and well regarded at UMC.

All three motorcycles represent what UMC's all about. As Watanabe says, "Some bikes are too original to restore or customize. Some are too far gone to restore. We try to honor each bike's history and build up whatever 'certain something' that it has."

That's a unique approach—as is the building from which UMC works. It's a dairy barn, built in 1896, in Nampa, which grew thanks to the Oregon Short Line Railroad constructing a track from Wyoming to Oregon, passing through Nampa. The barn was on the farm where Watanabe grew up. "My earliest memories were working and playing in the barn," he says.

"My father started milking cows out of it for a living around 1960," he says. "I had been dreaming about restoring it since about 1990. I have been into old bikes since 1985. Started

Union Motorcycle Classics' Mike Watanabe customized the 1973 Norton Commando Roadster that stands silent sentry outside their 115-year-old dairy barn in Nampa, Idaho.
Andy Stapper

At any proper motorcycle garage, work doesn't stop because the sun has set. Watanabe's father bought the property shortly after World War II and began milking cows in the barn around 1960. *Mike Watanabe*

Facing page: A Bultaco 250 Metralla—one of the great two-stroke pocket rockets of the 1960s—awaits further renovation. With the factory kit, they were formidable road racers as well. Watanabe found it in a scrap yard. *Mike Watanabe*

building customs in 1987. The barn seemed like a good fit, but my mother was using all of the space for storage."

Some time after Watanabe's mother died, he and partner Luke Ransom—"a professionally educated mechanic with very good fab skills," says Watanabe—figured it was time to launch UMC. "When Luke and I decided to open Union, the barn was a natural fit. It already had good power, heat, and a bathroom from the old dairy days. We first cleaned out all of stuff that was in it. We saved anything we thought could be reused. We then gutted the interior of the milking parlor, replaced all of the old electrical, and updated the plumbing. We then redid the interior and exterior with salvaged material from other old outbuildings on the farm.

"We basically approached the barn the same way we approach each motorcycle we work on. We assess what we have and make a decision on what is the best plan of action. We decided the barn would be much too expensive to restore to a pure 1896 version. We proceeded with restoring it like it was a hundred-year-old barn remodeled in the early sixties. We currently have the old milk parlor done and are working out of it. We cleaned the rest of the barn out last fall and are saving money to start restoring it."

Equally singular is UMC's organization. UMC consists of Watanabe, Luke Ransom, Bret Edwards, Andy Stauffer, and Jeff Barker. Ransom runs the day-to-day operations. Watanabe still has a day job in design, sales, and management with an unspecified corporation. "The shop is a studio for me," he says. "I see the bikes as rolling sculpture. The custom process is an art project for me. It is like creating a sculpture that you can ride when you are done.

"Bret Edwards is my longtime best friend. We have been building these old junkers together for almost 25 years now. We started building our own bodywork around 1990. I helped Bret start Glass from the Past. Bret fits into Union as a partner and supplier. I gave him a little advice on a bike he was building and a friendship was born out of that. We ended up spending a lot of time working on our bikes and helping others. This helping others is what started the idea of Union Motorcycle Classics. Andy and Jeff are support for graphics and Web. Both are vintage bike nuts." Or, as it says on UMC's website (www. unionmotorcycle.com), "Professional mechanics and restorers joining forces with professional designers equals something we like to think of as the Super Friends of classic motorcycles."

Ultimately, Union Motorcycle Classics brings the same formula to customizing and renovation (or not renovating) as it does to the barn it operates out of and the people that run it. It's a holistic approach that embraces a light touch, making use of what's available (and most valuable), and retaining, if you will, a certain patina.

And it's all happening in a 115-year-old milking parlor in Idaho.

Watanabe and friends refurbished the 115-year-old barn's milking parlor into UMC's work space. They plan to restore the rest of the barn as time and success permit. Watanabe was inspired by the barn-based garage of his late mentor, Robert K. Paull, who was a sheet-metal fabricator for the U. S. Air Force's SR-71 Blackbird. *Mike Watanabe*

Above: UMC has an impressive collection of vintage motorcycle toys—fitting, seeing as how a fascination with Mattel Rrrumblers helped fuel Watanabe's passion for motorcycling. *Mike Watanabe*

Above left: Watanabe's café-style custom Norton Commando Roadster. He tours on it occasionally, doing 600 to 800 miles. "Those 600 to 800 miles feel like 3,000 on a modern bike," he says. *Mike Watanabe*

Left: As you might expect, various historic impedimenta line the walls at UMC. The McCord Corporation of Detroit, Michigan, was famous not only for its oil seals, but also for making soldiers' M-1 and M-2 helmets during World War II. *Mike Watanabe*

The crafty little 1974 Yamaha RD60 is UMC partner Luke Ransom's project and shows their deft touch in restoration/renovation. The twin-stinger expansion chamber comes from Team Calamari Racing; the bodywork is from Glass from the Past, a close ally of UMC. *Mike Watanabe*

That's a BSA Gold Star in the foreground, a UMC customer's bike brought in for an appraisal restoration. Behind it is a Watanabe project, another BSA, but an A65 Daytona Replica. *Mike Watanabe*

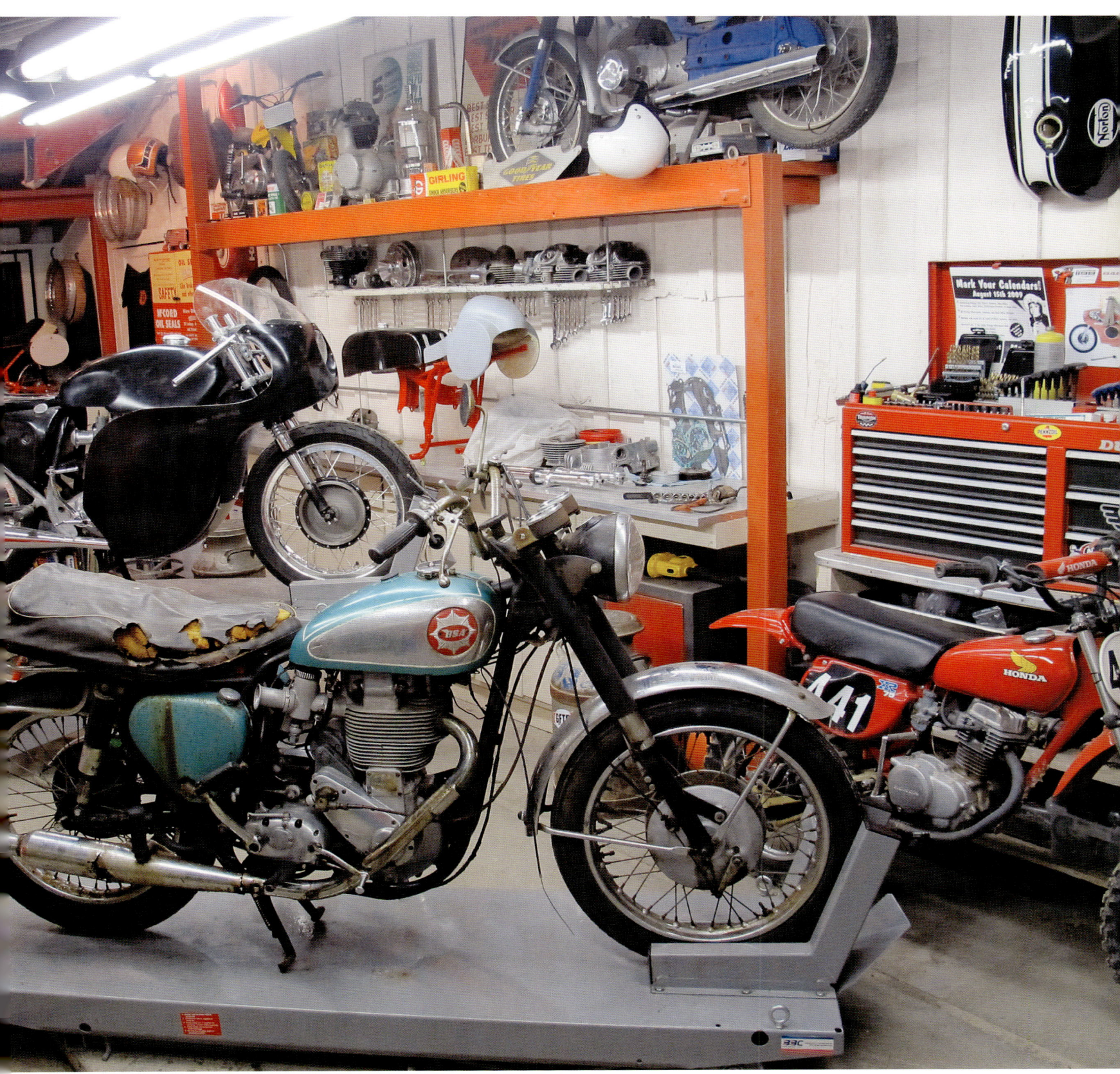

To the left is a 1967 Triumph TR6C Trophy 650, in for a tune-up. To the right, a Parilla Grand Sport awaits its turn to be restored. "It looks great from twenty feet away," Watanabe says. *Mike Watanabe*

> I see the bikes as rolling sculpture. The custom process is an art project for me.

The 1961 Triumph Cub is a perfect example of preservation trumping restoration. The wear and tear on the motorcycle is fitting and authentic—a rolling, rideable piece of fine art. *Mike Watanabe*

Above: Luke Ransom's 1963 Dodge van has an impressive ... patina, does it not? "The thing's a pain to drive, but it looks cool," says Watanabe. *Mike Watanabe*

Above left: The Husky racers of the 1970s and 1980s have a brassy appeal, with polished aluminum tanks and the splayed cooling fins of the two-stroke engine. *Mike Watanabe*

Top right: The barn that once held milking machines is now home to countless numbers of spare parts. *Mike Watanabe*

Left: Mattel Rrumblers introduced a generation of kids to motorcycles. Union's Watanabe was one of them. *Mike Watanabe*

part 4

SANCTUARIES

chapter 13

THE GRAND PRIX FAN'S HIGH-OCTANE DEN

Bob Bell's Eclectic Collection

BY ASHLEY WEBB / NEW ZEALAND CLASSIC CAR

WHEN YOU EXPLORE THE FUNKY CAR SHED OF KAIKOURA'S BOB BELL, it quickly becomes apparent that he has a great lifelong passion for cars to share—one that stretches back almost five decades to the time when he travelled to Ardmore as a child with his father to watch the NZ Grand Prix. In fact, Bob has been a keen motorsport follower ever since, not missing too many racing events at our end of the world—he's attended almost every Australian Grand Prix.

Bob has, quite literally, lost count of all the cars that he has owned over the years—although he recalled that it started at the tender age of 14 with a Ford 8. He remembers towing it home with his father and, after several attempts to get it running, they decided to wreck it—which, as it turned out, was quite a profitable exercise as the pair picked up a few bucks on the deal.

This was also the catalyst for what would play an important part in Bob's life—his shed. It was at around this time that Bob commandeered the family garage, and ever since he has always owned his own shed—and we're not talking your standard 6x6-meter job; every one of Bob's houses has boasted a decent-sized garage.

By the time he was 17, when Bob decided to head over the ditch (to Australia) to live, he had already owned at least a dozen cars, including a rare 1929 six-cylinder Chevrolet Roadster, three Model As, a couple of Austin specials, a Hudson Super 6, 1937 Tickford-bodied Rover drophead coupé—a car created especially for the 1937 London Motor Show—and a MkV Jaguar, the latter bought along with his father.

Unfortunately, Bob scuttled three telegraph poles in the Jaguar. With the eventual insurance payout, his father bought a 1949 Ford Single Spinner. Bob eventually saved up enough money and bought his own MkV Jaguar.

Bob lived in Australia for a while—he remembers that his first car over there was a Vauxhall Wyvern—but soon returned to New Zealand with his Australian wife. They didn't stay for long and were soon packing their gear and heading off across the Tasman again.

Initially, Bob purchased a Toyota Land Cruiser and a 6-meter caravan in which the couple travelled around Australia for just over a year. With their wanderlust slaked, the pair finally settled in Sydney.

Once there, Bob built their first house, which obviously included a fairly substantial garage. This would eventually house an early 3.0-liter BMW, a Jaguar XK150, a Lancia Fulvia Rallye coupé, a 1974 2.7 911 Porsche Carrera, and a VB SL/E Commodore.

The Lancia came to a sticky end when it took on a bridge and came off second best. The XK150 was sold, only to be replaced by a brace of Mk2 Jaguars and a rare 1961 Lincoln four-door convertible. A BMW 633CSi was added along the way, as well as a partially restored 1961 Thunderbird convertible—both of which he still owns today.

Bob recalls visiting a Sydney Motor Show in the 1980s and coming across the newly released Mercedes 190 Cosworth on display. Bob was mighty impressed with this car and wanted to get a closer look, thinking that this could be the car for him one day. Dressed in only shorts, sandals,

This vintage racer lives in the corner, along with a host of scale model cars, some tools, and a leather apron. *Adam Croy*

The garage of Bob Bell is the den of the dedicated, a place where Bell has spent decades collecting cars, parts, and interesting goodies. Pictured is a rare Alta/Vauxhall Special racer. *Adam Croy*

and a T-shirt (well, it was summer) he was refused entry onto the stand and not allowed to get anywhere close to the Mercedes. Bob then noticed a bright, shiny new BMW 635CSi on the stand opposite—the rest, I think you can guess; yes, Bob's also got a 635CSi.

During the mid-1990s, Bob and his second wife, Karen, travelled to Kenya to teach for six months after touring Great Britain and Europe in an old VW campervan. During that time, they adopted a 10-year-old Kenyan girl, Maureen. When they decided to return to Australia, the strict Australian immigration regulations imposed on them at the time meant that the easiest option was to return to New Zealand and fight the Australian authorities from there in order to get Maureen into the country.

That took around five weeks and, in the end, Maureen was only granted a five-year visa: if she left Australia during that period she would not be allowed to return. Bob and Karen decided to bring Maureen to New Zealand for three years, which would make her eligible for New Zealand residency.

Bob has fond memories of Kaikoura, having stayed there often while traveling over from Australia to attend classic race meetings. He and Karen had also spent time in Kaikoura over the years, and they decided to take Maureen to the South Island to see the snow, something she had never experienced before. During that trip they purchased a spectacular piece of land in Kaikoura that they had noticed on a previous trip. They then went back to Australia to sell up, which took about a year due to the length of time needed to sell their house.

Bob never told anyone in Australia about their new plans, other than to say that they were selling their house and building a new one—never mentioning that the new house would be built in New Zealand!

The ratty shed conceals some wonderful machinery, including this Jaguar Mark 2. *Adam Croy*

The Jaguar Mark 2 is a gorgeous, fast sedan and used a 3.8-liter XK6 engine. The Mark 2 was built from 1959 to 1967. *Adam Croy*

Above: The Morris Minor, stationary engine, and stuffed fawn exist harmoniously. *Adam Croy*

Below left: A Bathurst racing poster, old scale, and flathead cylinder head. *Adam Croy*

Below right: This vintage pump harkens back to days when gas station attendants—remember them?—sweated out a living pumping gas. *Adam Croy*

Bob also had to part with at least nine cars to lighten the load, including a rare 16-liter 1927 Le France fire-pumper. He was left with the Lincoln convertible, the Thunderbird, the BMW 633CSi coupe, an Alta Special vintage racecar, a Porsche Carrera, and a rare Benelli six-cylinder motorcycle.

And so, towards the end of 1999, Bob, Karen, and Maureen arrived in New Zealand and set to work building their new home in Kaikoura. The first challenge was to erect a temporary building so that they had a roof over their heads—this initial building would later become Karen's art studio and gallery.

The cars were kept in containers before Bob got around to building his large shed. Everyone still laughs, recalling that Bob built the shed before the house—but Bob's a man who clearly has his priorities set right. With the shed built and cars unpacked from the containers, it was time to focus on the house—which, incidentally, is fabulous. Its French provincial style allows for magnificent views of the surrounding mountains and sea from everywhere you look. Bob and Karen offer the house, now called Homewood Hill, as a luxury B&B for tourists who really want to spoil themselves.

Over the past few years since work on the house was completed, Bob has "sold a few and gained a few" as he puts it. He sold his 1974 911 Porsche Carrera and Lincoln convertible, replacing them with another Mk2 Jaguar, which has been built as a John Coombs Special. It boasts triple carbs, cut-out wheel spats, louvered bonnet, manual gearbox with overdrive, XJ6 rack-and-pinion power steering, and a Vicarage coil-sprung rear end.

The fully restored 1970 Morris Minor Traveller is Karen's daily driver. The unfinished Alfa classic racer, called the "Vault" due to its Vauxhall running gear—and the amount of money tied up in it—sits alongside a Thunderbird convertible, the 633CSi, and the Benelli motorcycle.

Bob's 1961 Thunderbird has since been modified to include a late-model Falcon rack-and-pinion steering, as the Australian RHD conversion was unacceptable for NZ compliance.

Unfortunately, Bob can't help himself when it comes to swap meets and visiting other people's sheds. Over the years, he has collected a substantial array of all kinds of motoring paraphernalia, including an impressive collection of old spark plugs. He's even got a penny-farthing bicycle.

As we wander around the shed, time seems to pass by quickly as virtually every item has its own unique little story, which Bob is only too happy to share. Naturally, there have been other cars that have come and gone, such as a Borgward Arabella coupé, a 1960s dirt-track racer, a couple of Morris Minors, a few Rover P6Bs, and a Triumph 2500 that Bob couldn't resist. Those cars have gone to make way for Bob and Karen's new plans.

Yes, the time has come for them to return to Australia. Maureen is now 21 and is building her own life in Auckland, so Bob and Karen have decided to head back over the ditch to be with family and friends. Although the decision was a hard one—which cars to take and which to leave behind—the collection will follow them and will, no doubt, take pride of place in Bob's next shed, wherever that may be.

> Bob built the shed before the house—but Bob's a man who clearly has his priorities set right.

If old vintage helmets could only talk, the stories they would tell... *Adam Croy*

Even though the garage was built in '99, there are areas which apprear untouched since the forties. *Adam Croy*

Vintage tools with vintage dust and probably a mouse nest or two underneath. *Adam Croy*

A Porsche 924 and Thunderbird convertible. *Adam Croy*

An Italian Benelli 750 Sei, which was produced in the early 1970s. Styling by De Tomaso was gorgeous, but a high price and limited availability kept the bike's production figures low. *Adam Croy*

A pile of plugs that will never again participate in a cycle of intake, compression, power and exhaust. *Adam Croy*

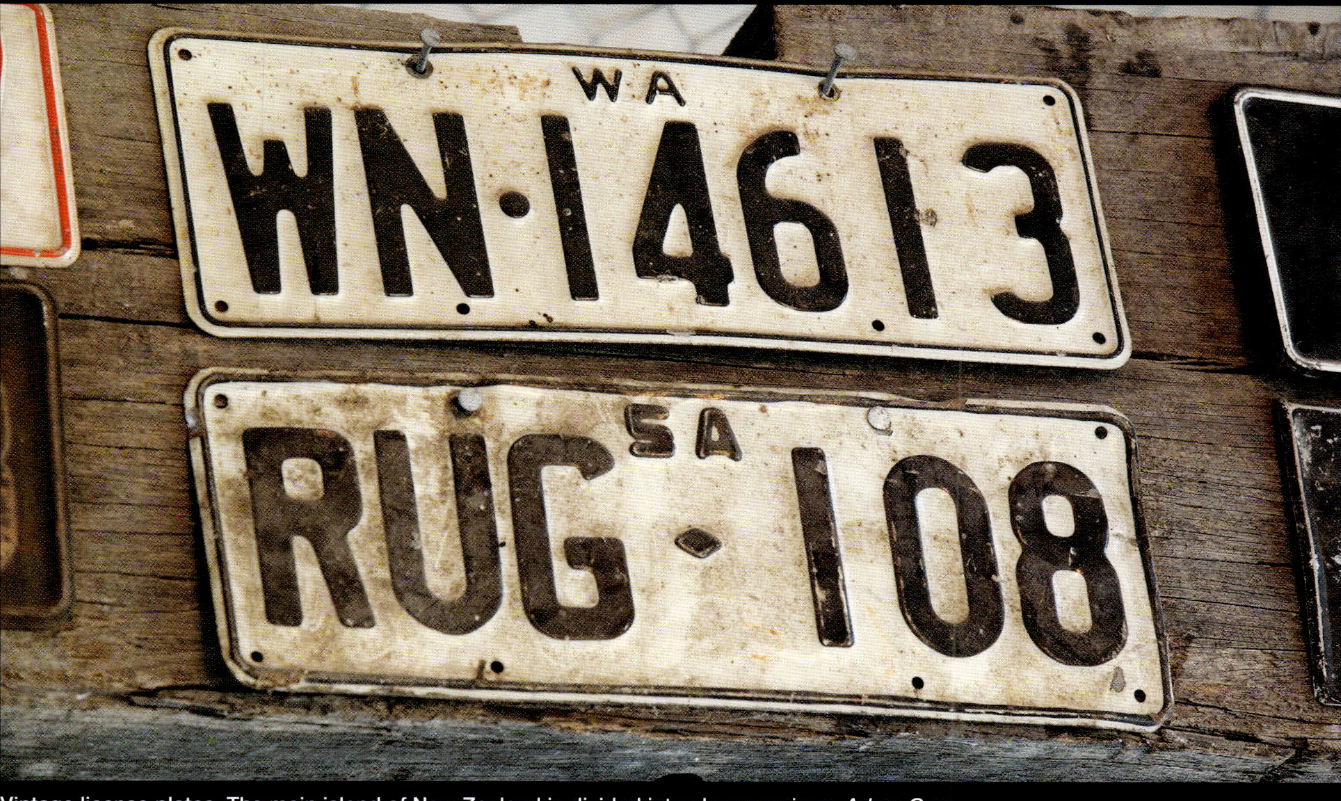

Vintage license plates. The main island of New Zealand is divided into eleven regions. *Adam Croy*

chapter 14
PILGRIM'S PLAYGROUND

The Motorsports Mecca of the Porsche Museum

BY CHRIS DAVIES OF WWW.THEIGNITIONPOINT.CO.UK

PORSCHE SPORTS CARS PRODUCE DIE-HARD DISCIPLES, millions as the years have passed. Their devotion called for some tribute, some sanctuary, where fans of the marque could gather, admire, and dream over the finest examples of Stuttgart's extraordinary handiwork.

There was a real and very obvious need for this place, for although the original Porsche works museum—which opened in 1976—was just a small offering and barely held 20 exhibits in rotation, it still attracted around 80,000 visitors per year.

But this new building is not a normal museum. It is not a musty, dimly lit place full of tired and hackneyed objects. Quite the opposite.

Porsche has built a "Museum on Wheels," continually expanding and changing the collection. Most of the cars on display will at some point participate in revival shows and races such as the Mille Miglia in Italy, Goodwood's Festival of Speed in England, and the Phillip Island Classic in Australia, to name but a few.

Fittingly located next to the factory in Stuttgart-Zuffenhausen, Germany, this is a building of ultramodern design, both inside and out. It is an edifice of clean-cut angles and straight lines—a lovely contrast to Porsche's curvaceous cars.

Viennese company Delugan Meissl Associated Architects beat 170 other architectural firms—and outbid the final 10—to win the right to design the building. Work began in October 2005, and the new museum finally opened in January 2009—right on time.

Part of the designers' philosophy is that "Inside and out, [our] concepts break down the order of conventional rooms into flowing, functionally defined spatial sequences."

Designed to be dynamic and bold—a reflection of the company's philosophy—the monolithic and floating appearance of the museum gives a sense of arrival and approachability. Like the company's iconic cars, it is unmistakable in appearance.

Instead of creating lavish and showy display areas, Professor H. G. Merz, who was responsible for the exhibition concept, lets the sports cars' own exceptional lines and presence speak for themselves. "Exhibits of this quality need no elaborate packaging," he says. "In Zuffenhausen, they stand like sculptures in a white gallery. Against these reduced surroundings, the visitor can be alone with the vehicles and with his or her own personal feelings."

Housed within the museum is the Central Department, containing the complete Porsche archives. Around 2,000 meters of shelf space accommodate materials covering everything from the first days of Ferdinand Porsche as a car designer to the complete cultural, social, business, and technical records that define Porsche AG. The archive includes over 2.5 million images, more than 1,000 hours of motion picture materials, and in excess of 3,000 books on various automotive subjects. This section is not open to the general public, but may be accessed by professionals such as scientists and journalists.

Many people know Porsche from its mid-century models and onward, beginning with vehicles

A collection of 1960s racing Porsches. Included here (top, right side) is the 1962 718 W-RS Spyder—nicknamed Grandmother for its long four-year racing career, helped by a robust 2-liter, eight-cylinder Boxer engine. It won prominent and historic races such as the Targa Florio and the 1,000km Nürburgring race. *Chris Davies*

like the 1955 Porsche 550 Spyder in which James Dean took his last drive. Professor Ferdinand Porsche's outstanding technical work dates back to the early twentieth century, however. From the beginning, he relentlessly pursued improvements to give his cars better performance and handling, a focus the company has never lost.

A key attribute of all Porsche sports cars is their favorable power-to-weight ratio. The beautiful 1922 *Sascha*, a car Ferdinand designed as technical manager for Austro-Daimler, effectively launched Porsche's great motorsport tradition, employing its power-to-weight advantage to secure 43 racing victories. Although its four-cylinder engine displaced only 1.1 liters, *Sascha*'s weight was kept down to an astonishing 598 kilograms.

Another important feature Porsche refined for his sports cars was aerodynamics. As a placard at the museum asks, "What good is 500 horsepower if it doesn't translate into speed? Making cars that are fast and still easy to control has been a chief objective since the days of Ferdinand Porsche. The key to achieving this goal is aerodynamic efficiency: the optimal relationship between desirable traction ('downforce') and undesirable drag."

Wind-cheating lines mark the 1939 Type 64, which is also on show. Again using the modest 1.1-liter displacement engine, it was capable of reaching speeds of around 80 to 90 miles per hour—a phenomenal velocity for the time. The graceful, flowing contours of the car not only embody Porsche's beliefs, they also project a vision of future Porsche models down through the generations. Can you see the beginnings of the 911 here?

Moving around the museum and on to the cars of the 1950s and 1960s, visitors can see the company's sustained emphasis on racetrack success. The Porsche 718 W-RS Spyder of 1962 used 2-liter, eight-cylinder power to dominate the competition over such a long racing career that its mechanics eventually nicknamed it Grandmother. Another car in the same section is the 1963 Porsche 356 B 2000 GS Carrera GT, dubbed Wedge Blade for its unique shape, evocative of an axhead.

Further on we enter the terrain of one of the museum's most recognizable forms, the road-going Porsche 911, a design that has not lost its definitive shape in over 40 years of production.

Facing page: The 1939 Porsche Type 64. Using only a 1.1-liter engine, it still achieved astonishing speeds of between 80 and 90 miles per hour. Opinions on its looks are often divided. For some, the car is ugly, yet others love its graceful and elegant lines. *Chris Davies*

A line-up of 1970s Porsche 917s in their various forms. Lightweight and massively powerful, their power output ranged from 600 horsepower to a colossal 1,400 horsepower, and some could reach up to 224 miles per hour on the racetrack. Many are remembered particularly, and fondly, for their liveries. Sponsors' colors such as Gulf Oil, Martini, and Shell tend to sharply stick in the memories of spectators. *Chris Davies*

Pilgrim's Playground **133**

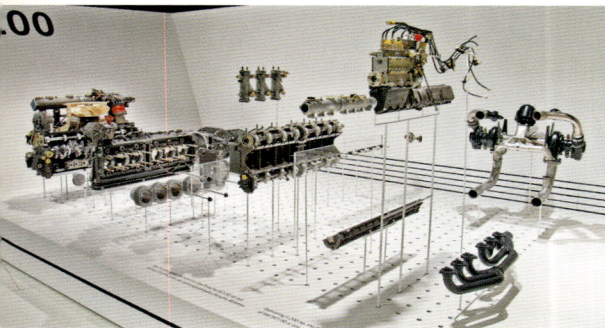

The split-down 12-cylinder engine of a Porsche 917/30. This is by far their most powerful race engine, producing a massive 1,200 horsepower. *Chris Davies*

Prominently displayed in this realm is the company's one-time flagship model, the 1975 911 Turbo 3.0 coupe, a car renowned for its braking, aerodynamics, and incredible-for-the-time 260 horsepower engine—qualities derived directly from the racing technology of the era. It was a fiercely fast automobile. As the Turbo edition evolved into the mid-1980s and gained even more power, it became a byword for raw, savage potency and ferociousness.

Continuing that theme, competition cars from the 1970s up to today in their familiar shapes and colors represent the cynosure for decades of race enthusiasts, representing extraordinary track performance under badges like Gulf, Mobil 1, Rothmans, and Martini.

Homologation rules benefitted a few wealthy fans in production models of the astonishingly expensive and exceptionally rare 959 from the 1980s and the 911 GT1 of the 1990s. These lightweight cars, bearing cutting-edge race technology, were hugely fast, capable of near-enough 200 miles per hour and barely street legal. They crouch in silver paint against black museum backgrounds that accentuate their aggressive and dilated bodywork.

The Porsche Museum is an architectonic wundercastle bearing the treasures of one of Germany's and sports-motordom's most revered companies. It is a garage for Porsche and for its droves of performance fans, an essential stop in Deutschland for any serious enthusiast.

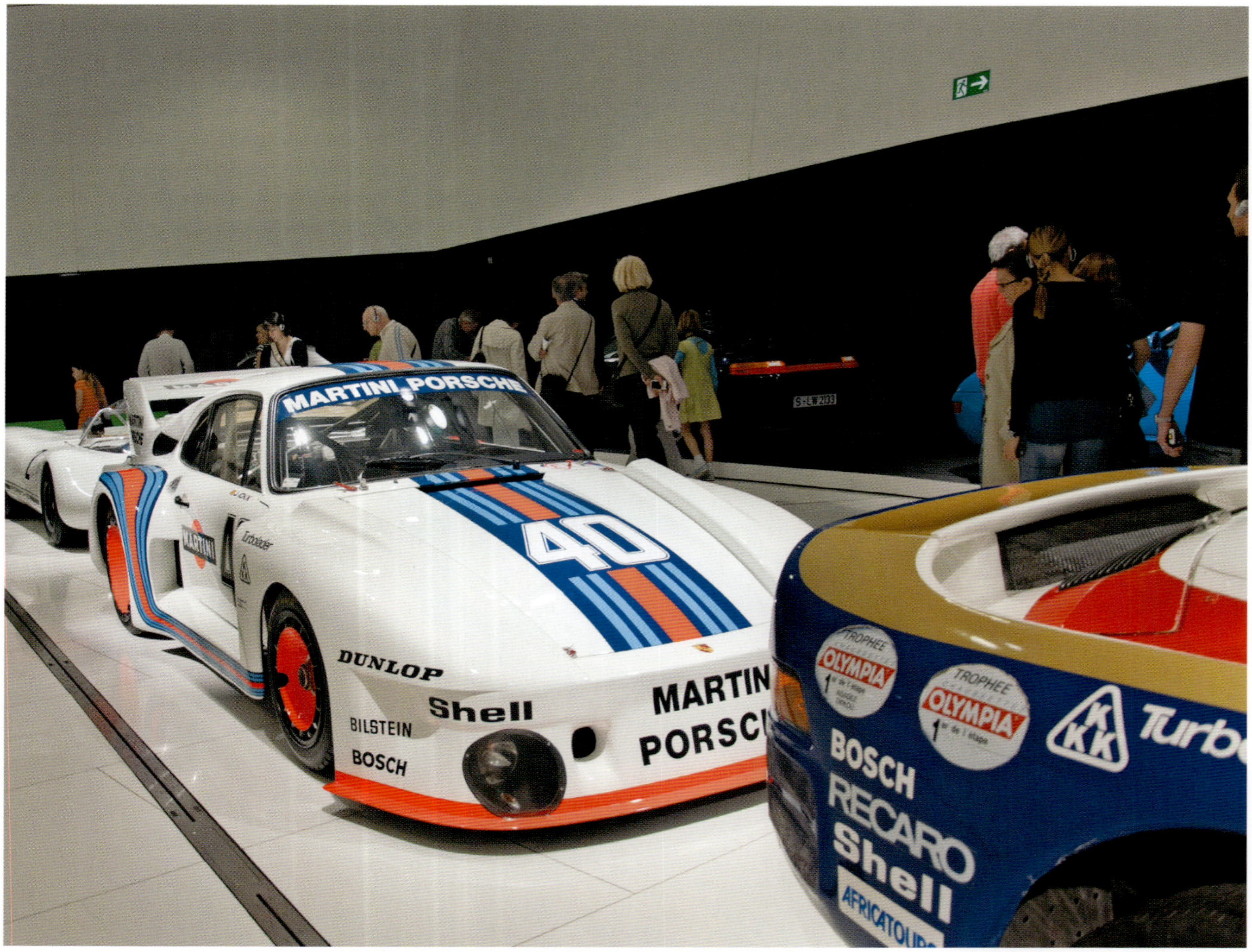

This Martini-sponsored 1977 Porsche 935/2 (center), nicknamed Baby, so dominated the World Championship for Makes in the 2-liter class that BMW withdrew from the competition. The car weighed just 730kg, including ballast, and had only a 1.4-liter turbocharged engine. Despite its small size, it still produced a remarkable 370 horsepower. *Chris Davies*

A 1996 Porsche 911 GT1 Straßenversion (foreground), and a Porsche Carrera GT. The GT1 is an ultrarare car. It was one of only 20 units built so that Porsche could comply with international racing rules. Its all-aluminum engine is a twin-turbocharged 3164cc Flat Six with around 544 horsepower and 442 lbs-ft of torque. *Chris Davies*

This 1951 Porsche 356 Light Metal coupe became part of the basis of Porsche's entry into motor racing. Its first outing at the Le Mans 24-hour race was rewarded with a class victory. Its little four-cylinder 1,488cc engine produced 70 horsepower and turned out to be very reliable. During one record-breaking 72-hour drive, it covered almost 11,000 kilometers at an average of nearly 95 miles per hour without incident. *Chris Davies*

Pilgrim's Playground **135**

Starting from the left, a Porsche-Diesel tractor, a model built from 1934 until early 1964; a Porsche 356 C 1600 SC Cabriolet, as used by the Dutch Rijkspolitie (highway police); a VW-Porsche 914/4, a collaboration between Volkswagen and Porsche in the late 1960s to the mid-1970s. *Chris Davies*

Weighing a mere 130 kilograms, this fiberglass-reinforced plastic body is taken from a late 1960s Porsche 908 "short-tail" race car. It would have had a fuel-injected 3.0-liter Boxer eight-cylinder engine with an output of around 350 horsepower. *Chris Davies*

A Porsche 911 GT1 98. Built on Porsche's 50th anniversary, this was the first time that a carbon-fiber chassis had been used. A double victory by the stunning GT1 was achieved at the 1998 Le Mans race. With 600 horsepower and a top speed of 217 miles per hour, this was a true monster of a race car. *Chris Davies*

The museum is an edifice of clean-cut angles and straight lines—quite the opposite of how Porsche's models look.

chapter 15

THE PORSCHE PALACE

The Southern Wisconsin Gearhead Garage of Thomas Grunnah

 **YOU WON'T FIND A STOPLIGHT IN ELKHART LAKE, WISCONSIN**—which is just how the 1,021 residents like it. The meandering country roads around the village wind through hills and dairy farms, and it's as green as the Shire in July, if not always as placid. Elkhart Lake's claim to fame goes back to 1951 and 1952, when sports car races were hosted on a street course near the town.

Racing on public streets is always a dicey event to keep alive, and the sponsors were not able to dodge the legal and political hurdles that such an event inevitably confronts. Fortunately, the need for speed was not snuffed out but rather redirected toward creation of a proper, race-only venue. Road America was built as a result of those races and remains one of the finest road racetracks in the world. As rolling and gorgeous as the streets of Elkhart, the track hosts a variety of prestigious events and races each year.

Tucked away just south of the blue-collar football mecca of Green Bay, the little town of Elkhart Lake became an idyllic escape for people from Chicago and Milwaukee, not to mention a haven for sports-car nuts. The streets sing with the sounds of Italian, French, and German sports cars, particularly when a club is hosting a big rally.

Thomas Grunnah came to Wisconsin in the mid-1980s when he and his family bought a hobby farm near Elkhorn, Wisconsin, not far from the Illinois border and only a few hours' drive from their home in the Chicago suburbs. Grunnah did his work in the city and spent as much time as possible on the farm.

The more time he spent on the farm, the more he came to realize something was missing. A farm isn't a farm without a tractor . . . so he started looking for one. It couldn't be just any tractor because devotion exerted its influence. Grunnah is a die-hard Porsche fan. In fact, he's owned a number of collectible cars, and almost every one of them is (or was) a Porsche.

"I bought my first Porsche in 1964," Grunnah said. "Thirty-five Porsches later, I'm still here."

So his natural inclination was to buy a Porsche tractor, which the company produced from 1950 to 1963—Ferdinand Porsche was experimenting with his design beginning in 1934. Ferdinand created a unique line of tractors that used single-, two-, three-, and four-cylinder diesel engines with interchange cylinder heads. The transmission was coupled to the engine via a hydraulic system designed for farmers accustomed to horses rather than engine-driven equipment.

After World War II, only German companies that had been producing farm tractors were allowed to resume production, so Porsche partnered with the German company Allgaier GmbH and Austrian company Hofherr Schwartz to bring its tractors to market.

In 1956, the restrictions were lifted and the tractor market was booming. Porsche bought the licenses back from the two companies and transformed the old Zeppelin factory into a tractor manufacturing plant. More than 125,000 Porsche-Diesel tractors were built between 1956 and 1964.

The small tractors weren't terribly popular in the United States. They didn't have enough horsepower for the market, and the exchange rate made them quite expensive. Only about

The Coupe is equipped with twin oil coolers, a roll bar, and a few other period-correct upgrades. Built to do the California Mille, the car is designed to be driven rather than shown.

The Porsche-Diesel Tractor Registry provides registration information and history for these rare tractors. More than 300 tractors are registered by the company.

1,000 of the little workhorses were exported to the United States. The model line ended with the 1963 year, with a few machines built in 1964. Porsche then abandoned the agricultural equipment business to focus on sports cars.

Grunnah searched for one of these machines not long after buying his hobby farm in 1990. He found one in Sarasota, Florida, listed not in a farm machinery catalog, but in *Panorama*, the magazine of the Porsche Club of America. The tractor had been imported into the United States by a member of the DuPont family.

"They brought three over from some farmer in Germany who was restoring them. One the DuPonts kept, one went to Vasak Pollak, the Porsche dealership on the West Coast. I bought the other one," Grunnah said.

The tractor was a 1960 Junior, the single-cylinder diesel model. It was in excellent but not completely perfect condition, which was ideal for Grunnah's purposes—he wanted a machine that could pull a wagon or do other light chores on his farm in Elkhorn. He bought it and had it shipped to Wisconsin.

"This one is in wonderful mechanical condition," Grunnah noted. "It runs flawlessly and never fails to start."

The tractor did light chores and also became an attraction at the Grunnahs' annual car event. They would invite a number of their friends to come over in their sports cars, and more than 50 cars would gather at the farm. The tractor was used to pull around a wagonload of kids and adults.

"It always gets a lot of comments, particularly in rural areas," Grunnah said. "People who are tractor savvy, when they see something with a Porsche logo, it blows their mind."

The tractor made appearances at a variety of events over the years, including the Walworth County Fair, which draws more than 150,000 people each year during a six-day span. "When

The Coupe, the Junior, and a 1967 Austin Mini Moke. The Moke is based on the Mini and was designed to be a competitor to the Jeep. The small wheels and low ground clearance didn't work off-road, and the vehicle was more widely used to haul guests and beach bums.

Not far from Elkhart Lake, Wisconsin, Thomas Grunnah's garage provides a genteel home for this nicely restored Porsche-Diesel Junior in a detached garage that is one of four on the property.

A 2001 Porsche 996 and a 2002 Maserati Spyder rest in the garage tucked under the back of Grunnah's house.

Grunnah is content to step outside his home and into his garage, where he can spin a wrench or two on a vintage machine, perhaps even take one down the lane and recreate a moment from those 1950 road races that made Elkhart Lake famous.

we were living at the farm in Elkhorn, the fellow who did the fence work asked if he could take it to local county fair. I told him, sure, you pick it up and you can do it. The tractor was a hit. There were some gorgeous tractors there, but everybody gathered around the Porsche tractor."

The tractor now resides on Grunnah's place near Elkhart Lake. Grunnah built that home in 2007. Prior to that time he had a garage near Plymouth, about seven miles away from Elkhart Lake. The garage was formerly the service area of a Chevrolet dealership, and it is a comfortable space to work on and store vehicles. But Grunnah wanted to bring his cars closer to his home, so he and wife searched out property.

Their favorite plot happened to be close to Elkhart Lake. The find was a happy coincidence for Grunnah, who has been visiting the sports-car racing mecca for many years. In fact, he'd attended the second street race, held there in 1952. The town's mix of small-town culture and big-town amenities suited Grunnah.

The garage houses a total of fourteen cars and has four separate spaces. One upstairs is for everyday parking, a space where four cars can be easily driven in and out. A driveway wraps around to the back of the house, where a tuck-under space houses four cars. A combination garage and living space is to the right of that, designed to house a show car and Grunnah's extensive collection of models and memorabilia.

The fourth, detached garage gives some additional space for cars. This is where the Porsche Diesel tractor makes its home.

Grunnah grew up with a love of cars and became enamored with VWs as a young man. His relationship with Porsches began in 1964 when he bought a lightly used 1964 356C coupe. "I knew nothing about Porsches," Grunnah said. "It bit me. I drove that car for a while."

Grunnah had the bug, and he bought and sold dozens of Porsches. One of his favorites is a 1956 Speedster that he has owned for more than 25 years. The car was a race car for most of its life and then was restored by well-known mechanic Jerry Leonard in the mid-1970s.

Grunnah has dabbled a bit on the racetrack but never got serious with it. His son, Tommy, made a serious run at racing in the 1970s and 1980s. He made it as far as Formula 3 racing, with Martin Brundle as a teammate, and ran some GTP races as well. Driving a Rousch car, he finished third at the Daytona 24-hour race.

Grunnah is content to step outside his home and into his garage, where he can spin a wrench or two on a vintage machine, perhaps even take one down the lane and recreate a moment from those 1950 road races that made Elkhart Lake famous.

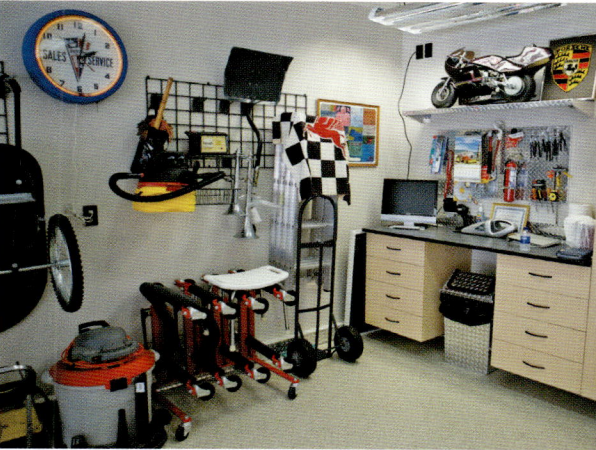

Above: Thomas Grunnah with his Porsches.

Top: This simple desk houses a few tools and goodies in the detached garage.

"Moke" is slang for donkey; they were built in the mid-1960s in the UK. Production moved to Australia from the mid-1960s to the early 1980s, and then to Portugal. Production was discontinued in the early 1990s.

Another wing of the house features this room housing collectibles and a 936 Junior. The car is a one-half scale replica of the 1981 LeMans winner built by Porsche. It has a Porsche serial number and manual, and you can order parts from Porsche for it. The cars were built to celebrate Dr. Porsche's 75th birthday.

Far left: This sitting room and bar is located just off the memorabilia room and offers respite to a car guy after a long day of wrenching, driving, or just soaking in that Porsche mystique.

Left: Grunnah's memorabilia collection is extensive and nicely displayed. He has more than 2,100 model cars.

The work space in the lower garage.

chapter 16

HOME OF THE SILVER ARROW

The Stuttgart Mercedes-Benz Museum

BY CHRIS DAVIES—WWW.THEIGNITIONPOINT.CO.UK

IN 1905, GERMANY'S LAST EMPEROR, WILHELM II, STATED, "I believe in horses; automobiles are a passing phenomenon." His countrymen were far better at building cars than the emperor was at playing Nostradamus.

Mercedes-Benz in Stuttgart, Germany, is the true home of the marque, one of the world's premier luxury manufacturers. Fittingly, it is here at the gates of their parent factory—and adjacent to the test track—that the company's new museum stands prominently on a hill in the Neckar Valley.

The facility was designed and built to harmonize the manufacturer's history with its ideals as a company. The old Mercedes-Benz museum was a three-story complex adjacent to the company's Stuttgart headquarters. It was last overhauled in 1985, and even with an update it still contained only enough space to exhibit a fraction of their automotive history. The new museum has enough space to house and properly display the company's entire 120-year automotive history—a unique achievement amongst car manufacturers.

UNStudio, founded by world-renowned Dutch architect Ben van Berkel, and the firm of Stuttgart-educated H. G. Merz were given the task of creating the wonderfully aesthetic building. Work began in 2001, and the design was fully realized in May 2006. Van Berkel had designed groundbreaking structures such as the Erasmus Bridge in Rotterdam and the Valkhof Museum in Nijmegen, while Merz had worked on the previous Mercedes museum update.

Aircraft-type polished aluminum strips intertwined with 1,800 triangular pieces of glass, each one unique, adorn the double-helix exterior design, while the interior of the building blends traditional and ultramodern—even futuristic—elements. The combination evokes the company's determination to use the best technologies available, while always pushing for advancement.

The museum is spread over eight levels. As van Berkel states, "It's really two buildings interlocking in a complex way. Because you've got these two spirals, it means at no point are they on the same level. You never know at which level you are, or where exactly you find yourself. Often visitors aren't quite sure whether they've actually been to a particular section." This novel layout gives the impression of a vast amount of space and makes patrons unsure of where the museum actually ends. Perhaps it's the designers' way of suggesting that Mercedes' history and goals have no insurmountable boundaries.

At the center of the museum is a triangular space that stretches from the ground floor to the roof. Three beautiful art deco–style elevators—reminiscent of the elegant trains of the 1940s and 1950s—travel silently up and down the three walls. As visitors rise to the top floor, giant pictures of former heroes, both cars and drivers, are projected onto the opposite wall, staying level with the elevator as it moves.

In the foreground is a 1908 Mercedes 75 PS Doppelphaeton. Only the ultrawealthy could afford such an extravagant automobile. Its massive six-cylinder 10,180cc engine produced just 75 horsepower and a top speed of 59 miles per hour. Furthest is a 1905 Benz 18 PS Doppelphaeton, which was the first in a series of new vehicles to take over from the old, taller models of the time. *Chris Davies*

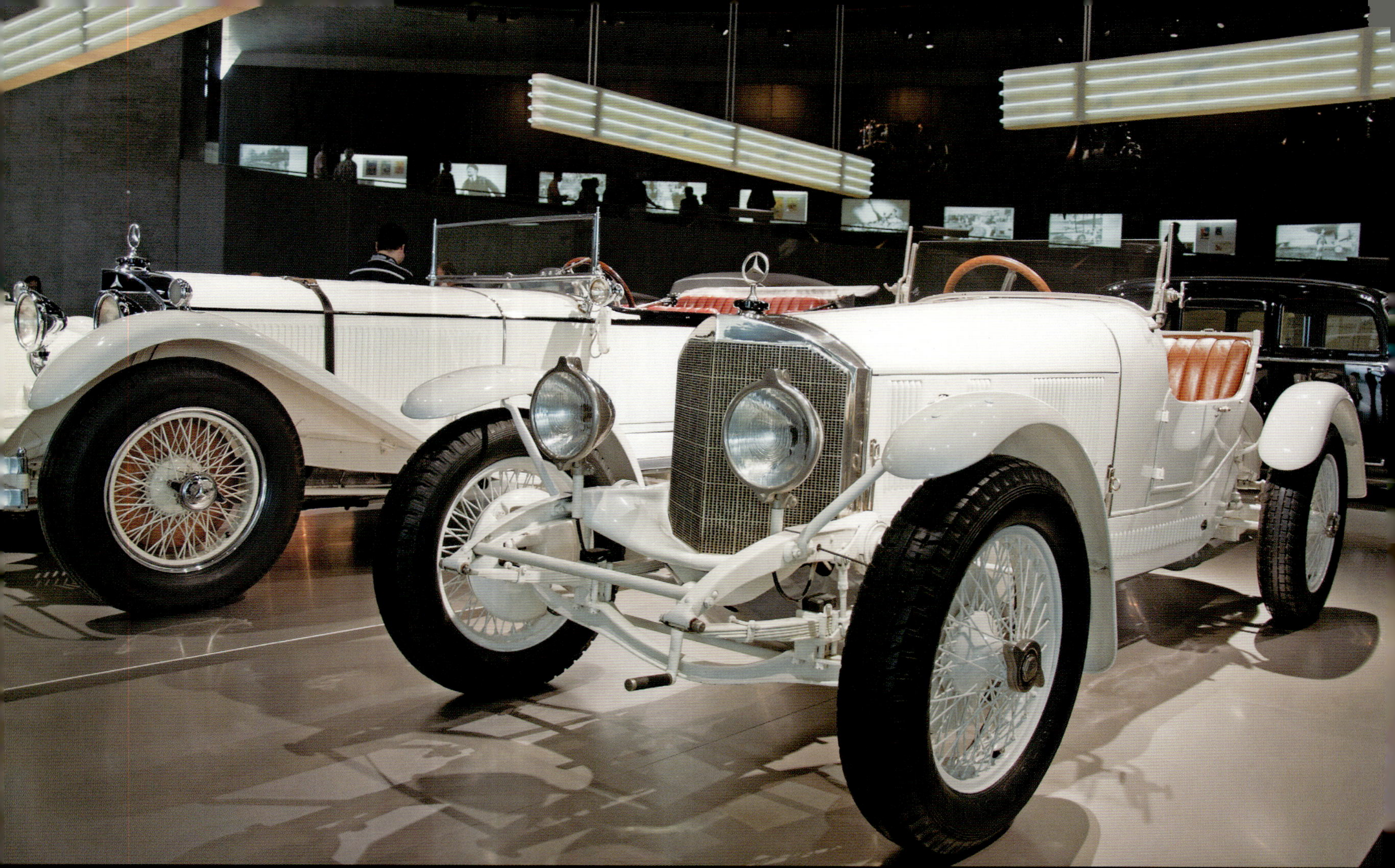

Nearest, a 1923 Mercedes 10/40 PS Sport-Zweisitzer. This was the world's first production car to feature a supercharger. Power from the 2.6-liter engine ranged from 40 to 60 horsepower. Next to it rests a 1928 Mercedes-Benz 26/120/180 PS Type S Tourenwagen, which boasted a 6.8-liter motor and a near-enough 100-miles-per-hour top speed. *Chris Davies*

The dashboard of a 1936 Mercedes-Benz 500 K Spezial-Roadster. Beautiful, elegant, and affordable only by the very wealthy, it featured a 5.0-liter in-line eight-cylinder engine with an ingenious switchable Roots supercharger to give extra power when needed. *Chris Davies*

The museum is a very large building consisting of 16,500 square meters of floor space. For some rest during their perusal, visitors can enjoy the museum's lounge, café-bar, and high-quality restaurant, all of which are automobile-themed. Some seating areas, for example, have built-in armrests of the style found in one of Mercedes-Benz' cars, and one of the eating areas features a wall-mounted display of some of Mercedes' pioneering vehicles. High above the tables you can see the solar-powered Alpha-Real Solarmobil, which was built in 1985 by a 21-year-old Mercedes-Benz mechanic. Also pinned to the wall is their E320 CDI diesel world-record holder, which covered 100,000 miles at an average speed of nearly 140 miles per hour on a closed circuit. The car was left in its record-setting state, still covered with the dirt and grime of a tenth of a million miles.

Over 160 vehicles are on display, and the diversity is simply staggering. Each is in near-immaculate condition, but rather than just being placed anywhere, they are grouped together into Legend Rooms and Collection Galleries, so that visitors can not only learn more about them, but also trace the history behind each vehicle.

Whereas exhibits at many official collections are cordoned off from the public by thick glass or velvet ropes, the Mercedes-Benz museum is barrier-free. Most cars have been placed on low platforms, allowing visitors free access to admire and scrutinize.

The Legend-Room vehicles are collected in eras, showcasing how their shapes and looks changed decade by decade. Early cars, such as the 1908 Mercedes 75 PS Doppelphaeton, have an aura of great opulence about them. With its 10.1-liter engine (621 ci) and a heady top speed of 59 miles per hour, that top-of-the-range model was available to only the ultrawealthy. Overly flared and curvaceous wheel arches were the order of the day, with plenty of highly polished brass on show and deep Chesterfield-like individual leather seats for the driver and passengers.

Moving on into the 1920s, Mercedes' cars changed shape. They retain an air of sumptuousness and grandeur but are more subtle than earlier models. Cars from the mid-to-late 1930s start to look more familiar, heralding more enduring shapes to come. The Mercedes-Benz 500 K Spezial-Roadster is one of these. Mercedes continued the trend of less is more, by fitting smaller engines, but imbuing them with greater power. When using the switchable Roots supercharger, the 500 K's in-line eight-cylinder 5.0-liter motor produced 160 hp—a massive capability for the period. Like its predecessors, it was a car for the rich and the beautiful, itself prepossessing and elegant, both on the exterior and interior.

Another Legend section presents the models of the 1950s. The 300 SL "Gullwing" coupe and its fellow Roadster and racing SLR versions represent some of the most alluring and captivating cars that Mercedes-Benz ever made. They are instantly recognizable to even the least knowledgeable of automotive fans. Although Mercedes carried on racing after World War II, due to limited resources they had to rely on the older "Adenauer" Mercedes, which were not competitive on the track.

The experience did serve to better Mercedes, for they could not command top-dollar prices for their road cars if competing manufacturers were leaving them behind on the racetrack. The company responded by developing an extremely lightweight (110-pound) tubular space frame and employing a direct fuel-injection system made by Bosch—a first for a production car. The 300 SL coupe could reach a prodigious 155 miles per hour, powered by a 3.0-liter straight-six engine, a truly amazing engineering feat.

Those 1950s SLs were sleek, sporty, fast—works of art in their own right. No wonder that in 1999, the Mercedes-Benz 300 SL was named Sports Car of the Century by an international jury.

Progressing down through the various levels in the museum, there is a huge amount to take in, as Mercedes-Benz are as proud of their other vehicles as they are of their cars. The amassed trucks, buses, off-roaders, car transporters, limousines, and racing vehicles are surrounded by countless thousands of Mercedes-Benz collectable items from bygone generations, reminders of how much affection people have for this truly outstanding marque.

As Mercedes-Benz continues to satisfy customers around the world with their superlative vehicles, so they also continue to indulge visitors with the ever-changing collection at their museum. Visiting the true home of the Silver Arrow in its birthplace at Stuttgart will far exceed any expectations one might have of what a museum should be.

The inner atrium of the Mercedes-Benz Museum. Art deco–style elevators on each of the three walls ferry visitors up to the top floor. This center section of the museum is also designed to funnel smoke out in the event of a fire. *Chris Davies*

This beautifully designed one-off rebuilt 1955 Mercedes-Benz Rennwagen-Schnelltransporter was used to chauffeur racing cars about, like the 300 SLR it is carrying. The Schnelltransporter's 3.0-litre engine gave 192 horsepower and a top speed of over 100 miles per hour! *Chris Davies*

The 1955 Mercedes-Benz 2,5-1-Stromlinienrennwagen W196 R. The name translated literally means "streamlined racing car." This magnificent and highly focused Formula One racer was capable of 190 miles per hour from just a 2,497cc engine. A huge achievement, even by modern standards of racing. The W196 R enabled Juan Manuel Fangio to win the 1955 Formula One world title. *Chris Davies*

Arguably one of the most iconic and memorable Mercedes-Benz automobiles ever made, the 1955 300 SL Coupe was fondly known as the Gullwing. It was a true supercar of its time. The 3.0-liter engine made 215 horsepower and would hit 155 miles per hour. The Gullwing door shape came about because a conventional door shape would not fit due to the SL's high frame side-members. *Chris Davies*

This now famed and legendary Mercedes-Benz Rennsportwagen 300 SLR was driven to victory by Stirling Moss, along with navigator Denis Jenkinson, in the 1955 Mille Miglia. Their average speed over the 1,597 kilometer race was an astonishing 97.9 –miles per hour—a record still not broken today! The 2,982cc eight-cylinder engine created 302 horsepower and a peak speed of 186 miles per hour. *Chris Davies*

The number *722* depicts the time that the car started the Mille Miglia race in Brescia: 7:22 a.m. Note that the car lacked any real safety measures, and that bare metal, wood, and glass dominate the cockpit. The drivers of the day were indeed brave men, as speeds would exceed 160 miles per hour and crashes would often be fatal. *Chris Davies*

This AMG-Mercedes C-Klasse DTM-Tourenwagen was the winning car in the 2005 DTM championship, driven by Gary Paffett. Its 4-liter V-8 engine produced 470 horsepower, equating to a pinnacle speed of over 170 miles per hour. *Chris Davies*

Center, the nose of an aggressive-looking 1989 Sauber-Mercedes Gruppe-C-Rennsportwagen C 9. With a 5-liter V-8 engine producing 720 horsepower and a top speed of 249-miles per hour, it enabled a 1-2 finish at the Le Mans 24-hour race, amongst eight other race victories that year and another five the year before, in 1988. *Chris Davies*

A selection of early race overalls. Compared to modern driver's suits, these are very antiquated. The clothing worn in the early 1930s consisted of heavy leather jackets and thin caps made of the same. Even into the 1950s, racewear offered little to no protection to drivers, especially if the car caught fire. *Chris Davies*

Nearest, the 1939 Mercedes T80. Featuring a massive 44.5-liter engine used in World War II fighter planes, it was tuned to around 3,000 horsepower. The 27-foot-long T80 was designed to set a land speed record with a target speed of 465 miles per hour, but due to the outbreak of war, this never happened. Furthest, the Mercedes-Benz W125 Streamliner. Over a flying kilometer, its V-12 5.5-litre engine propelled it to a colossal 268.7 miles per hour on a public autobahn near Frankfurt, a record still not broken since that day in 1938. *Chris Davies*

chapter 17

DOUBLE DECO

Mr. Smith's Second Helping of GarageMahal

BY CHARLES EVERITT

 **BY A CERTAIN AGE, WE KNOW WHAT WE LIKE.** Take, for example, Phil Smith, 73, retired from the air force, previously board chairman of Taser International, Inc., and now on a board of directors "who helps CEOs get their companies going," as he puts it. For his garage, Smith likes art deco artfully blended with high-tech to set off his collection of vintage gas pumps and his cars.

That's where Michael Rhodig and his company, GarageMahals, come in. To say Rhodig is a talented fellow is faint praise indeed. After getting his mechanical engineering degree in 1987, he worked in composite materials analysis and design at the Lawrence Livermore National Laboratory (a national security lab at Livermore, California, where they do not recruit second-stringers). In 2005, after pursuing additional careers in sales and marketing, software, and IT development, Rhodig founded GarageMahals, if not the first, then certainly the preeminent purveyor of luxury garage design and construction.

Rhodig knows high-tech materials and how to build with them. He is also a serious fan of art deco design. "It's an expression of math, power, and progress," he says. "That's what I see. It's about expressing 'newer, bigger, and faster.'"

Rhodig and Smith are so compatible that the GarageMahal featured here is their second collaboration; both structures are in Paradise Valley, Arizona, a town supposedly named by three surveyors from the Rio Verde Canal Company who were enthralled with the desert's beauty and tranquility. Smith's latest garage evokes the same feelings, but with harder and yet more ornate edges.

So, what did Smith request of Rhodig? "Basically, he knows I'm a pilot and a car collector," Smith says. "So, I told him, come up with something different, something art deco and high-tech, and incorporate airplanes. But art deco was the overriding theme I wanted when you walked into the garage."

"When it came time to do the second one," Rhodig remembers, "he asked for the same theme, plus much more."

Much more? Oh, yes. "I spent six times as much money on the second garage as the first," Smith says. "It makes the garage much more fun and usable."

The 1,500-square-foot garage features, of course, some of the usual suspects: big flat-screen television, a gleaming work space with a stainless steel–covered workbench atop double vertical rows of pull-out trays for tool storage. There's larger-item storage as well, but not of the conventional cabinet kind. Rather, it incorporates a signature feature of GarageMahals: rolling-door bypass cabinets, as Rhodig describes them. "Basically, what I created is a [non-structural] curtain wall of rolling doors I can put anywhere." They offer a flexibility in storage space you can't find in traditional cabinets.

Stars of this show include vintage gas pumps, unique composite doors adorned with historical aviation photos, and—most striking of all—the dramatic, exultant art deco columns

For his second garage from GarageMahals, Phil Smith asked for the same themes of art deco and high-tech—but jacked it up another notch. He got it, and then some.
Michael Rhodig / GarageMahals

The unmistakable face of Smith's 1953 SK120. "I saw one when I was 16," he says, "and always wanted one." He bought this right after meeting the car's former owner. *Michael Rhodig / GarageMahals*

The vaulting columns cover all the mechanicals for the garage doors, a staple of Michael Rhodig's GarageMahals design and one Rhodig says he originated.
Michael Rhodig / GarageMahals

that flank each of the doors. "Those columns, they're very cool," Rhodig says. "They've got these different elliptical shapes. Everyone sees something different in them." They, too, function as a bedrock element of GarageMahal's design, something Rhodig created. "I always use some sort of façade so you don't see the working mechanisms of the doors."

The doors themselves are quite special. Smith wanted his garage doors made from African mahogany, but their poor ability to weather Arizona's unrelenting sun created insurmountable problems. So Rhodig applied his high-tech materials background and designed them from foam-core, fiber-reinforced composites, finished to look like real mahogany. To hide the doors' interior faces and draw in the flying theme Smith wanted, Rhodig covered them with blown-up black-and-white photographs of 1930s Arizona aviation from the Ruth Reinhold Aviation Collection at the Arizona Historical Foundation.

At the other end of the garage, six flawless antique gas pumps—three Gilmores and one each from Texaco, White Eagle, and Polly-stand sentry below lighting façades that pay tribute to the awnings that once shaded true service stations. "Those are original gas pumps," Smith says. "We had to have one custom-built and had to go to a couple of shows to get parts. It took about 18 months to get them."

And what does Smith keep in his gilded palace of a garage? Well, not much these days, unfortunately. He still has a 2008 Mercedes-Benz SL550, a 2003 Bentley Arnage, a 2008 Chevrolet Suburban, and his wife's Rialta motor home, "to haul dogs around," he says. Sadly, his favorite, the 1953 Jaguar SK120 ("A fixed-head coupe, not a convertible," he insists)—the same model that thrilled him when he saw one at 16 years old, the one he later bought on the spot after meeting the owner—is gone. As are many of the others: the Porsche Turbo ("For kick-in-the-ass fun," he says), the Lamborghini Gallardo ("For 'meeting' girls"), the Lexus LS 600Lh ("For everyday"), the Bentley Continental GT, and the Mercedes-Benz SLR McLaren 722 GT. "I sold 'em off to stay afloat," Smith says. For a man with his accomplishments, it's unlikely the garage will have enduring vacancies.

Cars may come and go, but a man has few garages in his lifetime. Smith is glad to have chosen Rhodig for two of them. "He does everything," Smith says. "He's extremely creative, he's fun to work with; he's just an incredible young guy. If you look at the finish on this garage, it's exceptional. It's basically a turnkey job."

And how does Rhodig feel about his own design? "I think it came together well for what he wanted," he says. "I love the way it came out. There's a lot of different looks, a lot of different materials to create that look and feel."

Any regrets? Smith says he wishes he'd made it *bigger*.

Well, you know what they say: the third time's the charm.

Above: It took Smith almost two years to gather and refurbish his collection of gas pumps; one had to be custom-built. His only criticism of his 1,500-square-foot garage? He wishes he'd made it bigger. *Michael Rhodig / GarageMahals*

Top: Here you can see how skillfully Rhodig has combined the potentially disparate themes of art deco and high-tech. The red panels are another mainstay of GarageMahals. They're curtain walls with rolling doors for a remarkable flexibility in creating storage space. *Michael Rhodig / GarageMahals*

Left: Smith's collection of six antique gas pumps is integrated nicely into the overall design. In the foreground is a 1953 Jaguar SK120, which Smith has since had to sell. Behind it is a 2003 Bentley Arnage; he still owns that one. *Michael Rhodig / GarageMahals*

Above: The nerve center: The screen is for the house and garage security system. At left are the garage door controls. Keypad for the security system sits top-right. Below it are the garage's lighting controls. *Michael Rhodig / GarageMahals*

Top: The Gilmore Oil Company's Blu-Green gasoline was the firm's regular unleaded fuel. It also sold Ethyl (premium), Red Lion (regular, with tetraethyl lead), and Fleet (unleaded, low-octane for commercial use). *Michael Rhodig / GarageMahals*

Facing page: A pair of cases displaying memorabilia flanks the high-tech work station behind the Texaco Sky Chief gasoline pump. Above the pump is a lighting façade reminiscent of old service-station awnings. *Michael Rhodig / GarageMahals*

Much more? Oh, yes. "I spent six times as much money on the second garage as the first," Smith says. "It makes the garage much more fun and usable."

Another Rhodig tour de force. Smith originally wanted the doors made of African mahogany, but Arizona's climate ruled that out. Instead, Rhodig came up with fiber-reinforced composites over a foam core, with a near-as-dammit mahogany-look exterior.
Michael Rhodig / GarageMahals

Facing page: To reflect Smith's love of flying, the garage doors' interior sides feature images of Arizona aviation from the 1930s. Retired from the air force in 1963, Smith no longer flies. "My kids asked me not to fly anymore," he says. "They think I'm getting too forgetful. But it's probably for the best."
Michael Rhodig / GarageMahals

chapter 18

THE BEAST OF BUDAPEST

The Gazillion-Dollar Terminator-Styled Electric Mountain Bike's Stainless-Steel Palace

THE COMPOUND IN THE VILLAGE OF UROM IS NORTH OF BUDAPEST, in an area comprised of newer homes clustered among farm fields, located in the shadows of a low green mountain. After a short drive down Köbánya utca we pull into the cable, stainless steel, and glass M55 company headquarters. The place has a crisp, modern edge, with "M55 Bike" engraved in sans-serif type on the sign out front.

We knock on the front door to no avail, and my gregarious Hungarian guide, blogger Szilágyi Mihály (Mish), climbs the eight-foot-high metal gate, strides up to a black steel side door, knocks several times, opens it, and walks in. He's gone for some time.

Mish told me that the owner of the company was a well-known local developer with heavy-metal taste and a rock-star budget. He had decided that the world needed an electric bike and that he should be the one to create it. Not one to do things halfway, he hired a raft of engineers who spent five years developing an electric power-assist bicycle. I imagined a beefy Hungarian, skilled in the arts of backroom deals, who drove dark streets at 3:00 a.m. to clandestine meetings with a Murciélago on the pipe and off the grid.

I imagined such a man would not take kindly to entrepreneurial bloggers and opportunistic authors hopping over his fence to inspect his property. As my mental image turned to shotguns and bludgeons, the gate slid back electronically and Mish's head popped out of the door.

"Come," he said, waving his hand. "Is OK."

Inside I found a Spartan concrete workshop, the walls lined with steel racks holding plastic crates loaded with bicycle rims and tires and electronic components. A diamond-plate work stand in the center of the room held a chromed, futuristic bicycle. Two men were intent on the machine. A bald man in tiny wire-rim glasses and a hoodie hunched over a component he had hooked up to a laptop computer. The other man, Máté Megyeri, was a dark-haired thirtysomething wearing a red sweater zipped over a black T-shirt, three days' worth of five o'clock shadow, and a furrowed brow.

The shadows formed by my imagination and too much reading about Semion Mogilevich were wiped clean. The two men looked like any other young, intelligent, and slightly overwrought engineer you'd find making the machines that power our world.

Megyeri stopped his work and came over to greet us. He explained a bit about the M55 Beast. The bicycle was created with no expense spared. The owner hired the best engineers in the world—suppliers for Intel and BMW, to name a couple—and set out to create the world's best electrically assisted bicycle.

The bicycle evolved over a five-year period with three major prototypes built—The One, EVO-001, and The Beast. Each bike had more power and better control. One of the keys to this bike was the way it made power. The power is an assist—you have to pedal for the bike to go forward. But as you pedal harder, the bike responds with more power. The result is a sort of turbo-boosted bicycle.

The M55 Beast is an electrically assisted bicycle capable of more than 40 miles per hour. The exotic, hand-built feet-zap hybrid was designed by M55, a company based in Üröm, Hungary. Maté Megyeri is prepping the bike for an unveiling at the SEMA show in Las Vegas in October 2010.

The power is provided by an electric motor and 22 Tenergy lithium-ion battery cells. The combination provides up to 1.2 kilowatts of power—enough to move the bicycle along at up to 40 miles per hour and give it a range of between 75 and 150 miles, depending on output. The M55 Beast was built as a cross-country mountain bike with high-quality suspension components and tires.

The styling evolved as well, moving from the early design's Spartan, efficient look to the M55's Terminator Gone Wild heavy-metal-jewelry styling. "If Batman was a nonfictional person," the company website boasts, "he'd have a Beast in his garage for sure."

Particularly so if Batman's tastes switch from dark futuristic to blinged-out urban hip-hop. The M55 is anything but subtle, with a chromed exoskeletal-appearing frame accented by a gold drive wheel almost too pretty for a bike intended to go off-road.

Examining the bike in detail, Megyeri commented on the owner's dedication to quality. "We have the best guys in the world for this project," he said. "It's not about money. Much more about doing this by heart."

The heart of the owner is displayed in his company headquarters, an ultramodern space done in spare gray concrete and high-end trappings. Everything is crisp, modern, and the best. Steel cables accent the dark glass and granite. In one meeting room, a monolithic death's head leers down from the wall.

Eyeing the wall-mounted robotic skull, Mish said "He's a maximalist guy, no?"

"Yes. Right here, right now, and the best," Megyeri responded.

With that, Megyeri asked if I would like to ride the two bikes he had in the shop. One was a EVO-001 prototype, and the other was one of two rideable M55 Beasts. I did.

The EVO-001 was first, and pedaling the bike was interesting. The bike was slightly heavy but pedaled much like any other bike. As you increased the speed you pedaled, the bike provided some additional power. The power came on subtly, almost too much so. I knew I was going faster than normal, but not so much so that it was remarkable. I came off that bike wanting to try it out on a trail, as I suspected the power assist would be much more noticeable when scaling a nasty hill off-road.

The Beast was my next ride. Before I took off, Megyeri explained to me that the prototype was only providing half of the power of the final product. At lower speeds, the Beast provided a little extra jet of pedal power. In the higher gears, however, the assist became a velvet hammer. Down the slight incline in front of the M55 headquarters, the bike would squirt up to about 30 miles per hour with smooth, powerful acceleration. This felt like turbo boost, and I came back from the second ride beaming.

Megyeri needed to get back to work prepping the Beast, as he and the M55 crew were headed to Las Vegas to show the bike at the Specialty Equipment Market Association (SEMA) convention in a few days. But Megyeri invited me to join him and his crew at a video shoot of the bike in a square in Budapest.

At the shoot, I met Daniel Farkas, the company's press representative. Young, lean, and fluent in English, Farkas is a hard-core cyclist who—after some prodding—admitted that he permits himself to use public transportation only once a month. Everywhere else he goes, he rides.

Cruising through downtown Budapest on the electrically assisted Beast appeared to be great fun, and the bike has terrific potential as an urban commuter. Priced at 27,555 EU ($38,799) with a limited run, the Beast is a showpiece rather than an urban commuting solution. The next model is an urban commuter, the Daemon, and the slightly more economical model debuted at Monaco in April 2011.

The potential of power-assist bicycles is tremendous, and once these machines become affordable to the average human, both commuting and off-road riding will evolve and grow. Such technology could make 30-mile bicycle commutes more viable, and off-roaders could venture deeper into the backcountry.

For now, one Hungarian man with vision has created a technological jewel of a machine that allows ordinary humans to rip up pavement like Lance Armstrong. Let's hope the product of his lair in Urom continues to evolve, both for the sake of the sport of cycling as well as the limited supply of fossil fuel found on our planet.

> **Not one to do things halfway, he hired a raft of engineers who spent five years developing an electric power-assist bicycle.**

The M55 company headquarters serves as both the head office for the development of the electric-powered bicycles and the owner's construction firm. The Beast took five years to develop, with the technical design work contracted to some of the finest minds in electrical and mechanical engineering.

The modern building is environmentally friendly and high-tech, with a heating system integrated within the structure that uses air heat pumps. Huge 5-kilowatt solar collectors on the roof provide most of the power, and the interior lighting is done exclusively with LED lamps. An intelligent security system guards the building, so no human guards are needed.

The EVO-001 was the second major prototype, and the rear suspension system and frame design differ radically from those of the Beast. Engine power and delivery received similarly dramatic upgrades.

The computer controls on the Evo were on the frame, while the Beast's control system is on the handlebar.

The crank arm and power unit are custom-designed. The electric motor peaks at 1.3 kilowatts of power and is electronically controlled to match power delivery to the rider's effort. The complex system ensures that the power is delivered smoothly. Boost from the motor occurs only after the rider has made one-half turn of the crank.

The Beast has several different levels of power output as well as lights.

This piece of art was conjured up by the M55 team—they spent several nights brainstorming before commissioning the piece.

"As you pedal harder, the bike responds with more power. The result is a sort of turbo-boosted bicycle."

The office area for the M55 headquarters.

ACKNOWLEDGMENTS

Thanks to the contributors: Phil Aynsley, Gordon Campbell, Andy Catchpool, Adam Croy, Chris Davies, George Dzahristos, Mick Duckworth, Charles Everitt, Jim Haefner, Nick Lavigeur, John Noble, Michael Rhodig, Allan Walton, Mike Watanabe, and Ashley Webb.

Thanks to those who helped make this book come to life: Adachi Hiroyuki, Steve Casper, Paul DeRosier, Kristin Holder, Zack Miller, Kris Palmer, Nichole Schiele, and Jeffrey Zuehkle.

Thanks to all those who sent the emails and introductions that helped me find these garages, with special thanks to Szilágyi Mihály and William Hall.

Thanks to the garage owners who created the amazing spaces that appear in the book: Gordon Apker, Bob Bell, Rob Collett, Nagy Dóra, Jankó István, Thomas Grunnah, Giancarlo Morbidelli, John Pogson, Ray Rook, Phil Smith, Kazuo Ueda, Mike Watanabe, Fred White, and Robert Wirth.

A65 Daytona Replica, 116–117
ABC Skootamota, 58,
Alfa Championship, 108
Alfa classic racer, 127
Alfa Romeo Giulia Spider, 103
Allgaier GmbH, 139
Alpha-Real Solarmobil, 149
Alta Special vintage racecar, 127
Alta/Vauxhall Special racer, 124
AMC, 38
   Gremlin, 24
AMG-Mercedes C-Klasse DTM-Tourenwagen, 153
Anchorage, Alaska, 33
Apker, Claudia, 34
Apker, Gordon, 32–40
Arizona Historical Foundation, 159
Auburn, 33
Austin
   7 Special, 98-99, 101
   10 cabriolet, 74
   1800s, 24
   FX4 "London Taxi," 27
   Mini Moke, 140
   special, 123
Australian Grand Prix, 123
Austro-Daimler, 133
Aynsley, Phil, 53, 52–61
B-24 Liberator bombers, 38
Barker, Jeff, 112
Barr & Stroud, 87, 93
Barrett-Jackson Auction, 33, 36
Bathurst, 126
Bedford, 24
Bell, Bob, 122–129
Bell, Karen, 125, 127
Bell, Maureen, 127
Benelli, 55
   250/4 GP, 57
   250/4 Supercharged GP, 55
   750 Sei, 128
   6-cylinder motorcycle, 127
Bentley, 96, 98
   Arnage, 159, 160
   Continental GT, 159
   Speed Six, 36
Benz
   18 PS Doppelphaeton, 146–147
   see also Mercedes-Benz
Benz & Sohne, 101
Blitzkarren, 29
BMW, 24, 78, 123, 125, 127, 134, 167
   633CSi, 123, 127
   R12, 24
Borgward, 26
Borgward, Arabella coupé, 127
Borgward Blitzkarren, 29
Borgward, Carl F., 29
Borgward Hansa 1500, 28-29
Borgward, P100, 24
Bosch, 149
Bristol, 93
Brundle, Martin, 143
BSA, Gold Star, 116–117
BSA, Winged Wheel, 100
Budapest, Hungary, 7, 22–31, 166–174
Bugatti, 101
   Veyron, 43–45
Buick Special Riviera, 27
Bultaco 250 Metralla, 112
Burt, Peter, 93
Cadillac
   de Ville, 24, 26, 27
   Eldorado, 33
Campbell, Gordon, 70–75, 94–101
Catchpool, Andrew, 103–109
Centaurus, 93
Chevrolet, 7, 143
   C60, 31
   Corvette, 33, 36, 43
   Roadster, 123
   Suburban, 159
Chrysler, 39
Cicchello, Tony, 99
Citroën, 24
Classic Bike, 90
Coastal Motors, 71, 72, 73, 74
Collectible Automobile, 36
Collett, Rob, 87–93
Collett-White Mark V engine, 91
Concours d'Elegance, 107
Cord, E.L., 36
Corsa, 59
Corvair convertible, 69
Corvette, 33, 36, 43
Cosworth, 53, 67, 92, 123
Coy's Toys, 33
Cranch, Ivan, 99
Croy, Adam, 122–129
Cyclemaster, 100

Dacia 1300, 30
Daimler, 93
Darrin, Dutch, 38
Davies, Chris, 130–137, 146–155
Daytona 24-hour race, 143
de Havilland, 87
De Tomaso, 128
Dean, James, 133
Delugan Meissl Associated Architects, 131
Derbi 125/2 GP, 57
DesRosiers, Louis, 43–49
DesRosiers Architects, 43–49
DKW, 24
Dodge, 28, 72, 100
Ducati 125/4 GP, 56
Ducati 851 superbike, 55
Ducati 900SS, 111
Dunstall Norton Commandos, 111
DuPont family, 140
Dyke's Automobile and Gas Engine Encyclopedia, 66
Dzahristos, George, 45, 48, 49
Earl, Harley, 33, 36
Edwards, Bret, 112
Elkhart Lake, Wisconsin, 138–145
English Station Wagon Omnibus, 66, 69
Everett, Washington, 33
EVO-001, 167, 168, 170
Fangio, Juan Manuel, 150
Farkas, Daniel, 168
Ferrari, 43, 44, 102–109
   246 Dino GTS, 103, 104
   250 GTO, 107
   288 GTO, 103, 106, 107
   308, 104, 107
   308 GT4, 103, 107
   308 GT4 2+2, 107
   308 GTB, 106
   308 GTS quattro valve, 103
   328 GTS, 104, 109
   328 Targa, 103
   355 GTB, 103
   360 Modena Spider, 103
   360 Spyder, 13
   456 GTM, 103
   458, 107
   512 BB, 107
   Boxer, 103, 104
   Enzo, 103
   F40, 102–103, 104,106, 107, 109
   F355, 108
   Mondial, 103
   Testarossa, 103
Fiat
   509 Roadster, 101
   519, 95–96, 99
Ford, 23, 33, , 63, 100
   8, 123
   Deluxe woody station wagon, 40–41
   GT40, 43, 44, 45–47
   Model A, 63–64, 100
   Model A roadster, 54
   Model A station wagon, 63
   Model T, 63–69, 101
   Model T English Station Wagon Omnibus, 69
   Model T Ford Club, 64, 66
   Model T Touring, 69
   Mustang, 73–75
   Sierra Sapphire Ghia, 73
   Single Spinner, 123
   Tens, 72
   Thunderbird convertible, 123, 127, 128
Formula 3 racing, 143
Formula One racer, 150
Frazer, Joseph W., 38
Garage Life, 10–21, 76–83
GarageMahals, 156–165
GAZ, 24
GAZ M20 Pobeda, 27
General Motors, 24, 28, 36
Gilmore Oil Company, 159, 162
Glass from the Past, 111, 112, 116
GMC trucks, 24
Goodwood's Festival of Speed, 131
GP Mondials, 55
Grand Prix, 53, 56
Grunnah, Thomas, 138–145
Grunnah, Tommy, 143
GTP races, 143
Gulf Oil, 133, 134
Haefner, James, 43, 44, 45
Halley fire engine, 97, 100
Hansa 1500, 28–29
Hillman Imp GT, 73
Hispano-Suiza, 96
Hobbi, 24

Hofherr Schwartz, 139
Honda, 80–82
   350 Fours, 55
   CBR600, 55
Honshu Island, Japan, 76–83
Hudson
   Hornet, 37
   Super 6, 123
Hulme, Denny, 97
Husky racers, 119
Isotta-Fraschini, 96
István, Jankó, 23–31
Italia Autosport, 103
Jackson, Craig, 36
Jaguar
   Mark 2, 125
   Mk2, 123, 127
   MkV, 123
   SK120, 158–160
   X220, 107
   XJ-S convertible, 72
   XK120, 103
   XK150, 123
Jeep, 140
Jenkinson, Denis, 152
John Coombs Special, 127
Jones, Jeff, 99
K., Mr., 10–21
Kaiser, Henry J., 38
Kaiser Darrin, 38
Kaiser-Frazer Corporation, 38
Kaponga, New Zealand, 95–101
King, Roy, 95–101
Kiwi Metal Polishers, 74
Knight, Charles, 93
Lada, 24
Lady Wigram club car event, 73–74
Lamborghini, 103, 104
   Countach, 10–18, 11, 13, 18, 103
   Gallardo, 159
Lamm, Michael, 36
Lancia, 104
   Fulvia, 103
   Fulvia Rallye coupé, 123
   sedan, 33
Lawrence Livermore National Laboratory, 157
Le France fire-pumper, 127
Le Mans race, 135, 137, 153
Le Mans racer, 140
Legendary House Nagoya, 77
Lego Norton Commando model, 111
Leonard, Jerry, 143
Lexus LS 600Lh, 159
Lincoln, 123, 127
Linsdell, Steve, 87-89
Linto 75 Bialbero (DOHC), 56
London Motor Show, 123
M55 Beast, 166¬–171
Maranello, 103–104
Mark V engine, 91
Marquette Special, 98–99
Martini, 133, 134
Maserati, 42–49, 104
   Gran Turismo, 44, 45
   MC12, 43, 44, 45
   Spyder, 131, 133, 142
Mattel Rrrumblers, 111, 115
Maxwell, Charlie, 71
Maybach, 43, 44, 45
Mazda
   Miata, 78–79, 80–81
   Rotary Presto, 77
McCollum, James, 93
McCord Corporation, 115
McIntyre Matchless Grand Prix, 89
Megyeri, Maté, 166–174
Mercedes, 103
   10/40 PS Sport-Zweisitzer, 148
   75 PS Doppelphaeton, 146–147, 149
   190 Cosworth, 123-125
Mercedes- Benz 26/120/180 PS Type S Tourenwagen, 148
   T80, 154–155
   W125 Streamliner, 154–155
   see also Mercedes-Benz
Mercedes-Benz
   2,5-1-Stromlinienrennwagen W196 R, 150
   170V, 27
   300 SL "Gullwing" coupe, 149, 151
   500 K Spezial-Roadster, 148, 149
   E320 CDI, 149
   Rennsportwagen 300 SLR, 152
   Rennwagen-Schnelltransporter, 150
   Roadster, 123
   SL550, 159

SLR, 149
SLR McLaren 722 GT, 159
Mercedes-Benz museum, 146–155
Mercer Raceabout, 98
Merlin Spitfire, 104
Merz, H.G., 131, 147
MG, 63
   MGB, 64
   TC, 65
   TF 1500, 65
Miata, 78–79, 80–81
Mihály, Szilágyi, 23–24, 167–168
Mille Miglia, 131, 152
Mk2 Jaguar, 123, 127
MkV engine, 89
MkV Jaguar, 123
Mobil 1, 134
Molsheim monster, 43
Montesa Cota 25, 111
Morbidelli
   125 two-stroke GP, 53
   V8, 53
Morbidelli, Giancarlo, 52–61
Morbidelli Museum, 52–61
Morris
   Eight Series E, 72
   Minor, 126
   Minor Traveller, 127
   Minors, 127
Moss, Stirling, 152
Moto Guzzi, 59
Moto-Rêve 275, 55, 58
Munro, Barry, 96
Napier Sabre four-stroke engine, 93
Noble, John, 86–93
Norton Commando Roadster, 110–111, 115
Nysa, 24
NZeta, 100
Okato, New Zealand, 70–75
Oldsmobile
   F-88, 32-33, 36
   Golden Rocket 88, 24, 26
   sedan, 33
Oldtimer Park, 26
The One, 167
Opel Blitz, 28
Packard, 36, 37, 38
Paffett, Gary, 140
Panorama, 152
Paradise Valley, Arizona, 157
Parilla Grand Sport, 118
Paul, Robert K., 114
Pebble Beach Concours d'Elegance, 37
Pesaro, Italy, 52–61
Phillip Island Classic, 131
Pininfarina, 53, 104–105
Pobeda M20, 27
Pogson, John, 102–109
Pollak, Vasak, 140
Popular Mechanics, 33
Porsche, 43, 78, 107,130–145
   356 B 2000 GS Carrera GT, 133
   356 C 1600 SC Cabriolet, 136
   356 Light Metal coupe, 135
   356C coupe, 143
   550 Spyder, 133
   718 W-RS Spyder, 131
   908 "short-tail" race car, 136
   911, 133
   911 GT1, 134
   911 GT1 98, 137
   911 GT1 Straßenversion, 135
   911 Turbo 3.0 coupe, 134, 159
   911 Twin Turbo, 135
   914/4, 136
   917, 133
   917/30, 134
   924, 69, 128
   935/2, 149
   936 Junior, 144
   959, 134
   966, 142
   Boxer, 130-131, 36
   Carrera, 127
   Carrera GT, 133, 135
   Coupe, 134, 135, 139, 140, 143, 151, 159
   museum, 130–137
   Speedster, 143
   Turbo, 134, 159
   Type 64, 133–134
Porsche, Ferdinand, 131, 133, 139
Porsche Club of America, 140
Porsche-Diesel tractor, 136, 139, 140, 141
Ransom, Luke, 112, 116, 119
Renault
   12, 30
   Celtaquatre, 27

Rhodig, Michael, 156–165
Rialta, 159
Ricardo, Harry, 93
Rice Lake, Wisconsin, 23
Richardson Truck Museum, 97
Ridd, Ian, 97
Road America, 139
Rod and Custom, 33
Rolls-Royce, 39, 93, 96
   Crecy V12 engine, 93
Rook, Helen, 73
Rook, Martin, 74
Rook, Roy, 70–75
Rotary
   Cosmo, 77
   Kapera Sabanna GT, 77
Rothmans, 134
Rotorua, 74
Rousch car, 143
Rover drophead coupé, 123
Rover P6B, 127
Royal Aircraft Establishment, 87
Royal Enfield 125, 89
Ruth Reinhold Aviation Collection, 159
Sascha, 133
Sauber-Mercedes Gruppe-C-Rennsportwagen C 9, 153
Seeley racer, 89
Shakey's Pizza, 33, 34, 36
Shell, 133
Silent Knight, 93
Škoda, 23. 24. 26. 27
   440 Spartak, 27
   1100, 26
Slug Bug, 23
Smith, Phil, 156–165
Solex, 100
Specialty Equipment Market Association (SEMA) convention, 167–168
SR-71 Blackbird, 114
Stauffer, Andy, 112
Stipistop, 23
Stuttgart, Germany, 146–155
Subaru Leone 1800 coupe, 73
Sun Valley Classics, 36
Swiss Moto-Rêve, 55, 58
Sydney Motor Show, 123
Taser International, Inc., 157
Team Calamari Racing, 116
Tempe, Arizona, 36
Texaco, 159, 162–163
Tickford-bodied Rover drophead coupé, 123
Toyota Land Cruiser, 123
Trabant, 24
Triumph
   2500, 127
   Cub, 118
   Tiger Cub, 111
   TR6C Trophy 650, 118
Tsuchida, Takuya, 11
Ueda, Kazuo, 76–83
Union Motorcycle Classics, 110–119
UNStudio, 1471
Üröm, Hungary, 166–174
V12 750, 60
van Berkel, Ben, 147
Van Jac, 78, 80
Vauxhall, 87, 92, 124, 127
   Wyvern, 123
VB SL/E Commodore, 123
Veltex, 40
Vespa, 100
Volga, 24
Volga M21, 23
Volkswagen, 136, 143
   Beetles, 24, 26, 28
   campervan, 125
VW-Porsche 914/4, 136
Walworth County Fair, 140
Wartburg, 24
Watanabe, Mike, 110–119
Wawatosa, Wisconsin, 63
White, Fred, 86–93
White, Alice, 63
White Eagle, 159
Williams, Don, 36
Wirth, Alice, 63
Wirth, Robert, 62–69
Wirth, Todd, 64, 65, 66
World Championship for Makes, 134
X, Mr., 42–49
Yamaha RD60, 116
Yorkshire, England, 102–109
Zeppelin, 137
ZIL, 24